JUDITH

Bro. Lee

ISIKA

Asybit

D0952020

Sequoia-Size Success

UNLOCKING YOUR POTENTIAL FOR GREATNESS

Praise for Sequoia-Size Success

Sequoia-Size Success is an endless series of great ideas. It's a guide book for spiritual growth, and a resource for leaders, public speakers, pastors, parents and teachers. This book is priceless since it contains a depth of insight that could only come from wisdom Himself and a stream of practical principles that, if applied, makes the complexities of life easy. Thank you, Paul Tsika!

Ted Haggard, President
National Association of Evangelicals
Senior Pastor, New Life Church
Colorado Springs, CO

Paul Tsika's life resonates with every word he writes. His book will give you the basic root system to a life of fruitful success. All you add is the desire. Follow the steps. It will lead you to a life without regrets and success without sorrow.

Dr. Wayne Cordeiro
Senior Pastor
New Hope Christian Fellowship
Honolulu, HI

My good friend, Paul Tsika hits the nail on the head as he explains God's principles for prosperity in *Sequoia-Size Success.* This book of time-tested...rock-solid...never-fail...Bible-basics will show you how to get from where you are to places you've only dreamed of going. If your success isn't "sequoia-sized" perhaps it's time to get back to the basics of prosperity.

Tim Goad
Goad International

Paul Tsika does an awesome job of answering people's toughest questions about God's promises of prosperity. *Sequoia-Size Success* provides clear and carefully illustrated principles to help the reader grasp all that the Savior has in store for those who trust in Him. You will be blessed as much as I was.

Brad Duncan
Diamond, W.W.D.B.

You will be greatly encouraged by *Sequoia-Size Success*. This book has enormous depth and is a must-read for those who want to actualize God's plan to the fullest.

Terry Felber
Diamond W.W.D.B.

Sequoia-Size Success is packed with no-nonsense, don't-blame-anybody-else-for-your-problems facts about success. Throughout these pages, Paul Tsika brings profound wisdom that has been honed and proven through decades of corporate advising, personal mentoring and relationship counseling.

Greg Duncan
Diamond W.W.D.B.

Sequoia-Size Success

Unlocking Your Potential For Greatness

Paul E. Tsika

Plow On Publications

Scriptures are taken from the King James Version of the Holy Bible.

Plow On Publications
a division of Paul E. Tsika Ministries, Inc.
Restoration Ranch
5351 Hwy. 71
Midfield, TX   77458

www.plowon.org

Library of Congress Cataloging-in-Publication Data

Printed in the United States of America

This book is dedicated ...

To Ron Puryear, founder and president of World Wide Dream Builders.

Ron embodies the truths found in this book. His faith has been tried and he has come forth as pure gold. His commitments to do right have been challenged and he has stood firm. His True North principles have helped hundreds of thousands of people build a greater life.

He's loved and admired by those he leads.

He's a man of character and integrity, and one of the great leaders of this generation.

Although Ron is constantly in the public eye, he is a very private person who has a great love for family. He's a loyal and dedicated husband, a loving and caring father and father-in-law, plus an awesome grandfather.

He's also my dear friend.

Thank you, Ron for overcoming your doubts and fears to live out your dreams.

Brother Paul

ACKNOWLEDGEMENTS

I'd like to say thank you to some special people (because nobody writes a book alone):

Billie Tsika (my wife), who is my constant True North compass in life and greatest encourager.

Melanie Tsika (my daughter-in-law), who makes me look so good by taking bits and pieces and making them whole.

Paul Tsika,II (my son), for running my life and Restoration Ranch.

Cynthia Mackey, for organizing the layout of this book and providing the graphics.

Bill Hawkins (my friend), for his proof reading and correcting my outrageous grammar.

Plus, a special thanks to Wade Trimmer (my pastor), whose research, thoughts and ideas helped make this book possible.

TABLE OF CONTENTS

FOREWORD... BY JACK TAYLOR

J.H. Jowett has said, "Never trust a man without a limp." There are some limps that are external, more that are internal but just as real. Paul and Billie Tsika have been through the crucible and have emerged without the sight of singed hair or smoked flesh. Such are the fires of God.

I have known Paul and Billie Tsika for over twenty-five years, and after working with them, walking with them and weeping with them, I can tell you from my side of the room, they are real. What you see is what you get. What you hear is what they are.

I have always been amazed as I have watched them work together. He is stratospheric, she very deliberate and down to earth. He has a very effective accelerator, she has good brakes. He is the kite, she the tail keeping him steady. He is the dreamer, she the facilitator. Their singular commitment to Jesus and the extension of the Kingdom of God joins them together in a powerful compatibility born of attracting opposites.

While this book has been written by Paul it is because of this powerful merger of life and ministry that it is most effective. I love the subtitle, *Unlocking Your Potential for Greatness*. We have made a great deal of the issue of potential today as well we should. What we may have left out is the matter of its universality–it is in all of us! I have lived long enough to know that mere externals do not reveal the total picture of potential. I have seen those who could be described as "loaded with potential" crash and burn early in life while others who seemed "potentially challenged" rose to unimaginable heights and surprised all of us. This book quietly declares that we all have potential, that our potential can be unlocked and the procedure for that magnificent unlocking has principles which govern and enlarge the process.

While I am not surprised by the uniqueness of Paul's approach, I am rather surprised at the richness of such an obvious object lesson found in the great sequoias. Like Jesus, Paul has taken a matter in the realm of the natural and plugged it into the spiritual and applied to our lives in the practical. For that we are all indebted. The wisest among us are those who are able to take something commonplace and, bringing out the obvious and factual, carry us into an uncommon experience of discovering something within us that excites us about being here and being who we are. Most of us really lack such feelings about ourselves. This book can bring the reader to this conclusion: I am here; I am me; He is in me; I can dream; I can do. And I can expect results that I only previously expected to see in someone else.

The few pages that bring out amazing facts about the sequoia tree are central and should be read slowly if not again and again before proceeding to the remainder of the book. Everything that exists, that God created, holds such secrets, that when known, will change our lives for the better. The sequoia comprises a rich treasure for us all. As startling as are the facts about this great king of the trees are other attendant facts found throughout the book.

Paul has used several forms of communication which tend toward the facts learned in the book becoming permanent possessions, the use of acrostics (the statement of pertinent facts with words that begin with the same letter of the alphabet) being one. A strong example of this is found under Principle Five under the title of *The Secret of Abounding in Adversity*.

Other helpful acrostics used are typified in the incomparable acrostic on forgiveness under Principle Six as the way to properly handle our hurts.

As the book moves towards its climactic finish the next to the last division calls for us to make our success generational rather than simply contemporary. In other words Paul wants us to know that success by which following generations are not encouraged to succeed is not full success at all. We are enjoined to ask ourselves, "Am I preparing those around me to take the torch when I come to the end of my day?" What a statement: Success Demands a Successor!

At the end of the book (and this especially appeals to me as an exhorter) we are brought down to "crunch time", "paint or get off the ladder", "get with it or bail out". We are never to stop growing, ever-learning with the retained ability to think about the past without being chained to it and about the future without denying our heritage. My son pays me the greatest compliment I ever hope to receive when he says, "My dad never stops learning!" I really hope to come my day's end having learned a fresh truth that morning or late in the afternoon.

Paul, you have helped us all by your rich treasure of quotes from folks worth noting, your helpful puns, poems, euphemisms and catchy sentence structures that make us comfortable in being just us but terribly uncomfortable with the prospects of staying like we are.

I look forward to having the book in my library (the pay I receive from having written this foreword) and having it in the Frequently Trafficked section to which I often repair to stuff that "keeps me alive".

I predict for this volume a rapid and wide acceptance, a residual long life and a string of continued reports from readers of momentous and ongoing blessings.

Jack Taylor, President
Dimensions Ministries
Melbourne, Florida

Jack Taylor has written 13 books and is constantly working on two or three others. His first book, *The Key to Triumphant Living*, was a best seller, eventually selling upwards of half a million copies and still selling.

His book, *The Hallelujah Factor*, remains a standard resource in the area of worship.

When asked what his favorite offering is he alludes to his book The Word of God with Power which, he says, when believed will forever change the way we look at the Bible and ongoing illumination. He purposes to set straight what he calls the "hovering heresy", the idea that God used to speak to His people, wrote a book and and subsequently lost His voice.

In the intervening years between the first and latest of his books are those dealing with the family and marriage (*One Home Under God*), how to deal with the devil (*Victory Over the Devil*), how to walk in divine economy (*God's Miraculous Plan of Economy*), proper self-evaluation through God's eyes in Scripture (*God's New Creation*), living in revival (*After the Spirit Comes*), prayer (*Prayer: Life's Limitless Reach*), the inexhaustible riches available to all God's children (*Much More!!!*).

When asked what is the greatest book you ever hope to write, he replies, "The one I am working on now or the latest one I will write."

4

What is Sequoia-Size Success?

"Keep therefore the words of this covenant, and do them, that you may prosper in all you do." Deuteronomy 29:9

Use the word **prosperity** in most Christian circles and you will be greeted by snarls and hisses; not openly, but with a look, an attitude and possibly even a sincere rebuke. The very idea that God would want to prosper His people seems to be a contradiction to Biblical Christianity. "Christian Prosperity" with most believers is an oxymoron; an offense. After all, look at all the suffering believers around the world. Read the book of Hebrews or Foxes' *Book of Martyrs* and you see the idea of prosperity appeared to be foreign to their experience.

Does gain mean godliness or do riches equal righteousness? If one pastor has a large flourishing church and another a small struggling congregation, does that mean one is right with God and the other not? How about a healthy, fit brother or sister; and others who contract cancer or have a stroke or just plain suffer with physical challenges all their life? How about two Christian businessmen? Why do some seem to have the Midas touch and whatever they put their hand to turns to gold, but every time the other touches some-

5

thing, it turns to lead. Tough questions, tough issues, and apparently because of all the division among believers, even tougher to come to a Biblical balance.

On the one extreme, we have the name it and claim it, say it and seize it, blab it and grab it crowd. Right across the street (that seems to be across the world) we have the "God doesn't really mean what He says, so we don't have to confess, claim, or believe God for anything" crowd. They just let fate take its course. The only problem with both approaches is that they're both wrong, and headed for certain devastation. All the while, there's a road right smack dab in the middle of those extremes with a road map and guide to help stay on course.

The Kingdom of God is a kingdom of right relationships. How we relate in those relationships says volumes about our understanding of Biblical truth from God's perspective. Our Father has given us an abundant capacity to perceive, receive and achieve truth; His truth. The problem seems to be that we believers just don't believe. My observation about the majority of us is that we are professing believers and practicing agnostics. We say the Bible is God's word to us without any mixture of error, totally infallible. In other words, all of His promises to us are yea and amen in Christ Jesus. But, the writer of Hebrews reminds us of our responsibility. *"Let us therefore fear, lest a promise being left us of entering into His rest, any of you should seem to come short of it."*[1] We seem to come short

> *Our Father has given us an abundant capacity to perceive, receive and achieve truth; His truth.*

in so many areas of our lives as God's people. This results in many casualties along the highway of holiness; because of the great distance between His promises and our experiences. Frustration and confusion seem to plague us, defeat us and ultimately discourage us altogether from getting up and trying again.

I want us to soak in the promises of God and allow *His* truth not our experience to get deep into our spirit. A dear friend who mentored me in my early Christian life would reinforce to me over and over again: "Don't lower the Word of God to the level of your experience and try to make it fit, but repent and ask God to bring your experience up to the standard of the Word of God." Beloved, His Word is the standard. His Word is truth. His Word is ultimate reality. His Word is all powerful. All of our life the world has been trying to convince us that only what we can see, smell, taste, hear, or feel is reality. This only proves that *"that which is born of the flesh is flesh,"* but that which is born of the Spirit is spiritual. By faith believers can see things and hear things that the world can not. Faith transcends the five senses and without it, it's impossible to please God. The natural man, says Paul, *receiveth not* the things of God. *Receiveth not.* What a powerful phrase. The truth is, we waste our time, effort and spiritual energy trying to convince people who do not have the capacity to believe until they *become* a believer.

God's Word, God's Truth, and God's Promises are for God's people. Even though the principles of God's Word are universal in their application, like the rain that falls on the just and the unjust alike, yet, the *eternal benefit* belongs only to those who believe. A person may benefit in this life by applying the principles of God's Word to marriage, relationships, or business, because God honors His Word. However, reward *in this life* and the life to come apply only to those who not only trust the principles but receive the person of Jesus Christ as the Lord and Savior.

Every challenge that any person could ever face will find its solution in the Word of God. We need to understand that it is knowledge of and obedience to the Word of God that brings God's best for our life. There are three basic areas to deal with: the spiritual, the physical, and the material. We desperately need to know what God's Word to us is in each of these areas and be obedient to that word. We are spiritual beings who have physical bodies and live in a material world. God has a word for us. The prophet has said, "My people are destroyed for lack of knowledge." You've heard that old adage, "Ignorance is no excuse." But we say, "What we don't know, won't hurt us." Most people believe if they just turn a deaf ear to the truth, then it doesn't apply to them. Nothing could be further from the truth. God wants to bless us, God wants to use us, God wants us to prosper, but God will not violate His Word to accommodate us in our rebellion or ignorance. That's why the Word of God is replete with scriptures concerning obedience.

> *God's Word, God's Truth, and God's Promises are for God's people.*

You see, it's knowledge of and obedience to the Word of God that brings the best for our life. I am not inferring that if we know and obey, we will never have a challenge. However, we could all live on a much higher plane of pleasing God in our spiritual, physical, and material life than we do. For instance, if we have knowledge of and are obedient to God's moral law, it doesn't mean we'll never sin, but does mean we'll walk in greater victory than we do. Or, if we have knowledge of and are obedient to God's dietary laws (eating right, exercise, caring for my body) it doesn't mean we'll never have physical problems. It does mean we could live a healthier life physically.

What about God's material laws? In 90% of our counseling sessions there are financial challenges. We know the root is spiritual, but the fruit is often financial problems. Here again, it's knowledge of and obedience to God's Word that brings blessings. This does not mean we will never have a financial problem, but does mean we can have

> *We cannot violate God's Word in one breath and ask for His blessing in the next.*

greater material blessings and be more mentally content. We cannot violate God's Word in one breath and ask for His blessing in the next. God is longsuffering, patient and will work with us where we are. He will wink at things done in ignorance, as immature babies in Christ. However, He does expect us to grow up and accept our place as mature adults in the Kingdom and He holds us equally accountable. If you are having challenges in these areas, here are a few questions I've designed to help remind us of what we need to work on.

SPIRITUAL— What do you fill your life, mind, time, and attention with? What books, tapes, fellowship, do you allow into your life?

PHYSICAL—Your body is the temple of God. How do you steward it? Do you exercise? Are you overweight? What do you put in your body?

MATERIAL— Are you generous in honoring God? (Tithing and giving)

Are you frugal in your spending? Do you live below your means? Do you practice delayed gratification? Do you have a strategy to be debt-free?

The Word of God is like a walled city. In order to protect from the enemy without, it must confine to the parameters within. You can shout, "But I'm free," and tear down the walls that confine you, however you will then be exposed, to the enemies without. Our greatest and only freedom and liberty is to allow God's Word--God's truth--to be the parameter of our life. There are no limitations, there is only safety. For instance, financial prosperity like mercy is optional with God. God said..."*I will have mercy upon whom I will have mercy.*"—Also..."*It's God that gives the power to get wealth.*" Throughout God's Word, He gives mercy contingent upon the repentance of the person. He gives power to acquire wealth to those who are obedient to His Word and honor Him with obedience.

> *The Word of God is like a walled city. In order to protect from the enemy without, it must confine to the parameters within.*

We know that God is unlimited, unrestricted, and unhindered in all His capacities. It seems to me that we have hindered the Holy One of Israel in blessing us with the unlimited, unrestricted, unhindered benevolence of a father.

"Eye has not seen, nor ear heard, neither has it entered into the heart of man, the things which God has prepared for them that love Him." [2] I believe this verse speaks more of us in the nasty now and now, than in the sweet by and by. God wants us to be blessed NOW.

Some have the idea that money is the root of all evil. Plainly, it is not. Money has no morality. People who have it can use it for good or evil, to bless or to curse. It's the love of money that is the root of all kinds of evil. Whenever a person will lie, steal,

God wants us to be blessed NOW!

cheat, rob and by ungodly means seek to gain it; whenever a person loves things and possessions more than God or whenever we trust in uncertain riches more than the living God who gives all things freely to enjoy, that is the love of money ... *"it is good and right for one to eat and drink and to enjoy the good of all his labor that he takes under the sun all the days of his life, which God gives him: for it is his portion. Every man also to whom God has given riches and wealth, and has given him power to eat thereof and to take his portion, and to rejoice in his labor; this is the gift of God."* [3]

There is nothing that will bless the heart of a child of God more than knowing they are blessing God Himself. How do we bless God? The truth is too many of us spend our life robbing God of blessings rather than giving blessings to God. Let me explain. In scripture says, *"Will a man rob God? Yet you have robbed me. But you say, where have we robbed you? In tithes and offerings!"* [4] One day while reading that, I asked God a question. How can we as mere men rob you, the infinite

God who has need of nothing? God doesn't need anything. He's God! The answer to my heart was a revelation that has changed my life. The Spirit of God said, "Whenever you disobey my Word, you rob me of the opportunity of blessing you the way I want to bless you." There it was as big as life. When I rebel against or violate and disobey the Word of God in any area, I rob Him of the opportunity of blessing me with abundance. We can experience abundant joy, peace, life, faith, health (mental and physical), material possessions plus a whole array of good and perfect gifts that come from above when we obey God's word. God is blessed when I obey His Word in order that He might "open the windows of Heaven and pour out (on me) blessings there shall not be room enough to contain." This means I get full and then the overflow gets out to others.

> *Friend, God is looking us over for things He can praise us for, not condemn us.*

You see God will not disregard His own word to accommodate me in my rebellion. A father who blesses his children in their rebellion and disobedience only perpetuates the problem. Correction and chastisement must be enforced because you love them and want the best for them. The moment we repent, He runs to bless us with all the abundance He possesses. So, likewise our Heavenly Father looks for ways to bless His children. The scripture admonishes us to judge nothing before its time because God alone knows secret things and hidden things. And one day all will be manifest, *"Then shall every man have praise of God."*[5] Friend, God is looking us over for things He can praise us for, not con demn us. He wants to do us good, not evil, bless and not curse, help and not hurt. No wonder the sweet psalmist of Israel said, *"Oh the blessing, oh the happiness, oh the joys to the person who lives for God"* [6] David likens this person to a tree planted by the rivers of water. This phrase 'rivers of waters' translated literally means canals of water. The beautiful picture is that of being tenderly planted or placed by another right where you are. Right there where God has planted you is where He'll dig a canal to you and meet your every need. *"And whatsoever He doth shall prosper."* [7] Why? Because, he's been blessed, favored and loved by the God of all provision.

My prayer is that as you read through this book, you will think. Just think. Think about the God of Genesis and all that He created. Each time He brought something into existence, He said it was good. But, when He created man and woman the first thing He did was bless them. After that blessing, He commanded them to be fruitful and multiply, to replenish, subdue and take dominion. Dear reader, things may have gotten messed up for a while, but God put it back on track. He never reverted to plan "B." Plan "A" is still God's plan, and that plan is to bless us and not curse us.

My contention that God's plan has never changed can be reinforced throughout His writings. One passage has challenged me over and over: *"This book of the law shall not depart out of your mouth but you shall meditate therein day and night, that you may observe to do according to all that is written therein: for then you shall make your way prosperous and then you shall have good success."* [8] To me, God is simply saying, 'Believe, Understand, Do and I will prosper your works.' Your life will be filled with good success.

Most people would like to be successful provided it does not take too long, or cost too much time, money or effort. Unfortunately far too many have a segmented concept of success. In fact, they resemble the old farmer who had been ripped off many times by the used car salesman. Every time he went to trade vehicles the salesman would start his sales pitch by giving him the price for a basic car, then pricing each little feature on the car such as air conditioner- $200, Am/Fm radio- $75, whitewall tires- $50 extra, etc. One day the car salesman came to the farmer to buy a cow. The farmer got out his note pad and wrote: "One basic cow- $200, two-tone extra- $45, extra stomach- $75, dispensing device with four spigots at $10 each- $40, genuine cow-hide upholstery- $125, dual horns- $15, automatic fly-swatter- $35; total $535 dollars!"

> *Most people would like to be successful provided it does not take too long, or cost too much time, money or effort.*

Success, like the farmer's cow, is a package deal that cannot be segmented. A person could not be considered successful if he makes it big in business, sports, writing, etc., and yet is a failure in relationships with God and others.

Although there is a plethora of how-to books on success being offered today, most of them have a fatal flaw in that they spell success wrongly. A great many try to spell success M-O-N-E-Y. Others spell it F-A-M-E. Still others spell it P-L-E-A-S-U-R-E. This is the "farmer's-segmented-cow" definition and it's fatally flawed. The truth of the matter is that no person who has a lot of "stuff," or achieves a lot of fame, but leaves relationships out of his life is a success. No person who gives "much thought for his soon-to-die body and none for his never-dying soul" can be considered success-ful. No person can be

> *Someone said that success is a relative term – once you get it, all the relatives come.*

called successful who leaves any aspect of his whole being out of the picture.

Someone said that success is a relative term – once you get it, all the relatives come. A certain mountaineer was being examined for insurance. He had heard that any ques-tionable revelation about himself might eliminate the possi-bility of getting the policy, so he answered the questions cau-tiously. He answered the questions about his brothers and sisters with ease. But, when he was asked about his parents, he was alert. When asked about his father, he quickly replied, "He's dead." He was asked the cause of his father's death. Being afraid that he might lose the insurance, he replied, "I don't rightly know just exactly what it was that killed him, but whatever it was, it warn't nothin' serious!" One's defini-tion of success may not seem serious or vital, yet a mistake about it can be fatal!

Definitions of Success

Zig Ziglar writes: "Success is determined not by what you get for reaching your destination, but what you became by reaching it."

Mike Murdock defines success as, "the progressive

achievement of the goals God helps you set for yourself."

John Maxwell writes that "success is knowing God and His desires for me; growing to my maximum potential and sowing seeds that benefit others."

Dr. Ron Jenson states that "success is the progressive realization of all that you were meant to be and do."

My definition of success is: *"Discovering how God designed me to function and operating accordingly. Then I will be progressively developing into the person God designed me to be by directing the inner drives of my life to accomplish His goal for me."* Billie and I have tried to instill in our children one thing from the time they could understand. That is, success from God's perspective has more to do with faithfulness than results. The world says "bring home the bacon," "rise to the top," "Be #1." But over and over again we are admonished to steward the life afforded us by being faithful to grow into the person we were created to be. We have a mission statement at World Wide Dream Builders. The last part of that statement sums it all up for me. It simply says "God created man for greatness."

We are blind until we see that in the human plan nothing is worth the making if it does not make the man.

Edwin Markam said, *"We are blind until we see that in the human plan nothing is worth the making if it does not make the man. Why build these cities glorious if man unbuilded goes—in vain we build the world unless we know the builder grows."*

Bill Cook underscores the fact that *"Success is much more than a matter of achieving the right things; it's also a matter of being the right person."* Thus, we see that success is not a position one concretely arrives at, but a process one continually adjusts to in order to be all that God designed us to be and to do all that God desires us to do. It lies not in achieving what you aim at but in aiming at what you ought to achieve.

By now you are probably wondering with all the books on the market informing us as to the methods and principles of success, why one more? Because few, if any, have been written using the principles gleaned from the Biblical analogy of the "Blessed Man" being like a tree. We read, *"Blessed (prosperous, successful) is the man who does not walk in the counsel of the wicked or stand in the way of sinners or sit in the seat of mockers. But his delight is in the law of the LORD, and on his law he meditates day and night.* **He is like a tree planted by streams of water, which yields its fruit in season and whose leaf does not wither. Whatever he does prospers."**[9]

If the "blessed man" is like a tree, then principles gleaned from the largest in size and

> *The giant sequoia trees should give us keen insight into destiny fulfillment and dynasty achievement.*

longest living things on earth – the Giant Sequoia trees – should give us keen insight into destiny fulfillment and dynasty achievement. Would you not agree that anything that has managed to not just survive, but thrive in the midst of a harsh environment through centuries of drought, storms, fires, lightning strikes, and the lumberjack's ax, and has lived to be from 2,600 to 3,500 years old, must have some great lessons on successful living to teach us?

If we can harvest the fruit of Biblical principles gathered from these giants of nature and apply them to our lives and vocations, we too can have SEQUOIA-SIZE SUCCESS! The Giant Sequoia stands literally as a monument to overcoming odds and obstacles fulfilling the great purpose for which God created her. This is His plan for your life.

I pray you will be blessed, encouraged, enlightened, informed and inspired. I pray that you will be, not just successful, but that you will have SEQUOIA-SIZE SUCCESS!

Paul E. Tsika

Amazing Facts
about Sequoia Trees

While you are wandering through these forests of facts, I want you to read them in light of your own relationships. Trials, adversity, struggles, growth, and survival are only a few of the pictures painted for us by this magnificent tree. Take your time and enjoy the tour.

Picture a tree taller than the Statue of Liberty. Picture it larger around and through than a Greyhound bus. Imagine this tree just beginning to sprout when the Pharaohs of Egypt started construction on the pyramids some 3500 years ago, and you begin to see how truly amazing is the oldest and largest living thing on earth.

Technically the proper name for the giant sequoia tree is Sierra Redwood and its Latin label is Sequoiadendron gigantean, i.e., giant sequoia.

C.J. Horn tells us how the trees got their name: "The December 1996 Good Science Botany Column examined the process of assigning botanical names to various plants. In the case of the Redwood trees, this process has taken some interesting turns! In 1769 a Franciscan missionary accompanied a Spaniard expedition and mentioned "red wood" trees in his journal. In the next 100 years, these trees were examined and named by Scottish, English, Austrian, American and French botanists. Each discoverer tried to name the trees in such a way to convey their characteristics and awesome greatness: Taxodium sempervirens (an "ever living" member of the cypress family); Wellington gigantea (after the Duke of Wellington); Washingtonia californica (after President George Washington). In 1776, Pedro Font, awed by the trees, named one palo alto ("tall tree"). A town founded on this site still bears the name of that tree. John Muir called the trees "Kings of Their Race."

The Austrian Stephen Endlicher was the first to assign the tree to a new genus— Sequoia. Some say this was due to his great admiration for Sequoia, the Indian. The genus Sequoia was finally adopted (instead of Taxodium) and in 1938, John Buchholz did a thorough study of the two types of redwoods and noted the differences between them. He named the redwoods that grow on the foggy northern coasts of California and southern Oregon Sequoia sempervirens (sempervirens means "ever living). He named the giants of the Sierra Nevada Mountain groves Sequoiadendron giganteum. For general purposes, the trees of the coast are referred to as Redwoods, while the trees that grow in the Sierra Nevada groves are called Sequoias."

The giant sequoia grows on the western side of the Sierra Nevada Mountains in 75 groves in an area 260 miles long and 15 miles wide. Its bark is sometimes as much as 4 feet thick, with 50 feet long branches that begin some 100 feet up on the tree. These trees have survived for 2 or 3 thousand years, some even longer. Some of the largest of these trees measure 45 feet in base diameter and up to 300 feet in height. The tallest standing giant sequoia is 311 feet tall. They can grow up to 1 to 2 feet tall per year until they reach between 200 to 300 feet high. Some sequoias weigh ten times the size of the largest animal on earth – that being the female blue whale.

The sequoia tree grows almost anywhere, but will only grow to its greatest size at elevations of 6,500 feet on the western side of the Sierra Nevada Mountains.

Several factors contribute to the incredibly successful long life of the giant sequoia. Among these is its astounding ability to come through forest fires, in many instances without even being scarred by the fire. Due to its unusually thick bark, which is fire-resistant, the sequoias actually depend on fires to thin out the firs and pines that would otherwise eventually take over. Likewise giant sequoia seeds do well in a fire-mineralized soil, and in fact, need the heat of the fire to cause the release of their seeds from the cones in the most prolific numbers after the fire.

Another amazing fact is that a typical fire in a sequoia forest leaves no marks on the giant trees! Their branches begin at a height of 100 feet, so there is no chance for the fire to reach them. The trees lack the flammable resin typical of other trees, which makes them fireproof if the fire moves fast enough through the underbrush. However, if the fire is hot enough it will burn into the trunk of one of these giants. The fire will leave a charred wound, but the tree begins immediately to repair the damage. In the growing season following the fire, the tree will grow slabs of wood thicker than the bark on the rest of the tree in order to cover the burned portion.

The tree also contains a natural wood preservative and is very resistant to disease. It has the ability to ward off disease or insects. In fact, it has been said that "no known disease will kill a mature redwood." No one knows how long a redwood/sequoia can live. This unique ability of the redwood/sequoia tree to withstand fire and disease and insect attack accounts for their long life span.

A typical Redwood/Sequoia forest contains more biomass (Biomass is the mass per unit area of living plant material. This includes both roots and shoots) per square foot than any other area on earth, and that includes the Amazonian rain forests!

Sequoias have remarkably shallow roots. There are estimates that suggest that 95% of these trees have roots no deeper than 3 feet! Despite their shallow roots, sequoias are resistant to toppling because their roots spread out over large areas, sometimes up to half an acre in well-drained soils. Also, they grow in groves with other sequoia with which they intertwine their root systems, thus providing mutual support for each other.

The Coastal Redwoods/Sequoias thrive on and in fact require the heavy fogs that are normal daily occurrences along the coast. These 300-foot plus tall giants actually pull moisture into their needles at the tops of the tree where the circulation system of the tree can't pump. The 50-60 degree average temperature of the area is also important to the life cycle of these trees. Due to these two conditions, restrictions are placed on the modern day range of these awesome giants. Although they will grow almost anywhere in America, they will never attain their true size and stature without the Coastal fogs and temperatures that nurture them and at the same time keep other competing species, such as pines, stunted and sodden.

Another amazing fact about the sequoia/redwood is its desire to go on living even if it gets knocked over. A fallen sequoia will attempt to continue growing via its limbs. If undisturbed, the limbs pointing up will turn into trees in their own right, and this is indeed the source of many row groups of trees.

The redwood/sequoia burls (a burl is a large rounded outgrowth on the trunk or branch of a tree) are another survival strategy. Their growth is held in check by the presence of chemical signals in a living sequoia. If the tree should die, or even be stressed by low rainfall or fire, the chemical signal weakens or vanishes and the burl will burst forth into verdant life. Burls kept in a shallow pan of water will grow almost indefinitely. They can also continue on to become a full-grown redwood/sequoia tree.

A major contributing factor in making the redwood/sequoia tree such a success as trees go is its unique ability to survive rising soil levels over their immense life spans. One particular sequoia, known as the coastal redwood, has the ability to grow roots at the surface, thereby overcoming rising ground levels that are commonly brought about by flood deposits. These deposits typically smother other trees' root systems, killing them. The coastal redwood simply grows a new lateral root system! Seven successive layers of roots were observed on one fallen redwood meaning that the ground level had risen dramatically up the tree seven times and each time the tree responded with a new root system. The total rise on this particular tree was 11 feet over the trees 1200+ year life. It has been observed that some 1000+ year-old redwoods have experienced and survived rises in ground level of as much as 30 feet! Couple this with the sequoia's ability to survive long periods of immersion and their immense durability in the face of flood borne debris and you will realize that the redwood can survive and indeed thrive in flood planes that wipe out less hardy tree species.

The Coastal Redwoods compensate for induced leans caused by shifting slopes, collisions of other trees, flood pressure and tectonic-induced tilting by the unusual ability to "buttress" their undersides through accelerated growth on the downhill side. It is possible to find groves of trees all leaning in the same direction!

These amazing characteristics make the sequoias stand apart from the rest as well as providing many clear and cogent principles for successful living with SEQUOIA-SIZE SUCCESS.

Principle One

Don't Despise Small Beginnings!

"Do not despise the day of small beginnings." [1]

If Sequoiadendron gigantean (giant sequoia) could talk, it would probably state up front that the first principle of successful living is: **"Don't despise small beginnings."** The giant sequoia tree's cones are tiny compared to a grown tree. In fact, it is only about the size of a chicken egg. The seeds are even smaller. Each seed is only the size of a flake of oatmeal!

We live in times in which if anything or anyone starts out small or few, it is considered laughable and is disparaged. If it isn't massive in numbers, mighty in influence; if it isn't big, beautiful (and brawny); if it isn't large, loud and lauded by the masse—it isn't considered worthwhile.

Everyone who got where he IS had to begin where he WAS using what he HAD.

Have you noticed how very few people are willing to start where they are with what they have? Normally they wind up never doing anything because they cannot begin big and powerful. They go for broke and start up with an impressive show, the big venture, the spectacular splash, only to fizzle in the end. They want to capture the attention and admiration of as many people as possible as quickly as possible. This is the American way for the most part, but it is not God's way. He begins everything He does in a small way; with a seed, an idea, a word, a baby, sub-atomic particles, atoms, etc. With proper cooperation with His design and laws, growth, increase and steady progress come to fruition.

One day a salesman visiting a small rural town in Alabama stopped on the outskirts. He saw an old gentleman sitting on the porch in a rocker. Curious about the town and trying to get a feel for the people, he asked the old man a question. "Hey Neighbor, just wondering, any famous people born in this town?" "Nope," came the reply, "just babies." The truth is that's how we all start, just babies. The key is to try to not stay that way all your life.

> *Everyone who got where he IS had to begin where he WAS using what he HAD.*

Our Creator God builds living things on the principle of the tiny seed. Like the giant sequoia, we all came from a very tiny seed. A seed is a living pattern, a genetically coded structure that under the right circumstances will reproduce its parent, with unity in diversity.

A good seed is a word, a pattern, a vision, a picture, an idea for changing creation to conform to God's design. A bad seed is a word, a pattern, a vision, a picture, an idea for changing creation into a state of confusion against God's design.

26

Principle One: Don't Despise Small Beginnings!

From the sequoia we learn that seed power and growth isn't equal to the size of the seed. If you were to be given an oatmeal flake size giant sequoia tree seed, you could never know by initial and outward appearance that you held in your hand something that had the potential to become the largest and longest living thing on the earth. What seems so insignificant to the world has the potential to impact the whole world.

The principle of not despising small beginnings is graphically illustrated years ago by a demonstration in the Chicago Museum of Science and Industry. A greatly enlarged checkerboard was displayed on the top of a table. In the first square of the board (the lower left corner), one wheat seed was glued there. In the second square, there were two. In the third square, there were four, and the number was doubled in each succeeding square. However, the process was discontinued after the eighth square and the squares of the rest of the board were empty. A large plaque in front of the exhibit explained the reason.

The eighth square was completely covered with wheat seeds, and there was no room for more. If the process had been continued all the way to the 64th square (doubling the number with each new square), there would have been enough wheat seeds to cover the entire sub-continent of India fifty feet deep!

So what if you were born on the wrong side of the tracks; so what if you had such a poor and painful childhood; so what if your business is small. You and your business or career have the potential to achieve greatness in God's sight if you know that it all began with the right kind of seed.

John F. Munro, in an article entitled, "From Small Beginnings Come Great Things" writes: *"Often referred to as the 'backbone of our Nation,' small businesses are heralded as one of the main reasons for the economic success of the United States. The U.S. Small Business Administration contends that small businesses 'create two of every three new jobs, produce 39 % of the gross national product, and invent more than half the Nation's technological innovation. Our 20 million small companies provide dynamic opportunities for all Americans.'"*

A message from Hayward Wesleyan Church bulletin read:
"Do not despise small beginnings.
Every giant redwood started out as a little seed.
Every skyscraper began with a shovel of dirt digging down to go up!
Every eagle hatched from an egg, and every butterfly from a cocoon.
Every best-selling book and blockbuster film started as a thought.
Every grand invention began as a little idea.
Every good marriage started with a small glance and a smile.
Every great hero used to be a little baby.
Every world record musky started as a tiny fish egg!
Every heart-stirring song began with a single note.
So -- the world of small seeds, little ideas, single notes and fish eggs is the place where true greatness is born!

Do not despise small beginnings -- they contain the
magic of wonderful hopes yet unfulfilled."

In its first year the Coca-Cola Company managed to sell
only 400 bottles of Coke. It was a small beginning. That's less
than 5 bottles sold in a week. Today the success of Coca Cola
is hard to dispute. Coke is sold in more than 195 countries
and is consumed 773 million times in a single day. Revenues
are in the range of 20 billion dollars per year. Small beginnings have great potential don't they?

Microsoft's founder and multi-billionaire, Bill Gates said:
*"Pick an area because you really think you can contribute some-
thing unique and because you enjoy working on it every day.
And that's where
you'll be able to do
world-class work, the*
*Do not despise small beginnings --
they contain the magic of wonderful
hopes yet unfulfilled.*
*best work in the world.
And it starts with very
small beginnings. You
know Microsoft never thought of itself as a big company. At any
time we always said, well maybe we could double in size. If
things went perfectly, when we had 100 employees we thought
maybe we could have 200. And so we were very cautious about
how we spent money and how we thought about building up our
organization, so we find ourselves really surprised as we look
back on these 25 years at how far that's come."*

William Wilberforce, the Englishman responsible for
almost single-handedly stopping the slave trade in England
wrote:

"Things great have small beginnings.
Every downpour is just a raindrop;
Every fire is just a spark;
Every harvest is just a seed;
Every journey is just a step because
Without that step there will be no journey;
Without that raindrop there can be no shower;
Without that seed there can be no harvest."

We should not underestimate anything small in quantity, size or number. This is because small things have incredible potential for both constructive as well as destructive results.

A case in point of a little thing being destructive is found in the story of Robert Leech of Manchester who shot to fame when he went over the Niagara Falls in a barrel. Nineteen years later he died slipping on a piece of orange peel in Auckland, New Zealand. He escaped the great and was caught in the small. This can be true spiritually. We can do great things for the Lord, but fail to maintain God's basic standards. King David escaped the paw of the bear, the mouth of the lion and the hand of Goliath, only to be defeated by his unrestrained passions.

The old saying is true, "little is much when God is in it!"

Author Ken Gire has a prayer that stresses the importance of little things. He writes:
"Dear Lord,
*Teach me not to despise small beginnings. For it was in Bethlehem, the least among the cities

of Judah, that you chose to start your life on this earth.

*Teach me the meaning of little things. For a mere cup of water has eternal significance when given in your name.

*Teach me the value of little things. For a widow's mites are the true treasures of heaven.

*Teach me to be faithful in little things. For it is by being faithful in little things on this earth that I will be given responsibility for greater things in your kingdom.

*Teach me the far-reaching effects of little things. For a simple request by a crucified thief ended up changing his destiny for all eternity.

*Teach me the power of little things. For how silently the mustard seed grows, yet how pervasive is its influence; how invisible the yeast works, yet how transforming is its power..." It was only a little stone taken from the brook, but in David's sling it became the first guided missile that brought down a kingdom.

> *I would rather live life with those who attempt great things and fail than with those who attempt nothing and succeed.*

It was only a little lunch from a young boy, but in the hands of Jesus it became the source of sustenance for thousands. It was only a little bottle of perfume, but when poured out on Jesus its fragrance filled the room and beyond, and its remembrance transcends 20 Centuries.

And amidst a world so big we seem so tiny and insignificant, but He still values little things, knowing that in His hands they accomplish great things as dreams are realized. The old saying is true, "little is much when God is in it!"

People may belittle your small beginnings.

Your Legacy

Throughout my life, my friends and folks have offered
    me advice.
And though they meant the best for me, it often wasn't
    nice.

They'd always say my plans and thoughts were just more
    crazy schemes;
and every time I listened, I let them steal my dreams.

I guess they feared, in case I failed, that I really
    shouldn't try.
And so I never spread my wings and I never learned to
    fly.

But they're just folks who only see the world and
    all they blame.
And I'm no longer content to let those people cause me
    pain.

So I'll abandon myself to what I know may seem to be
    extreme.
But I'll leave behind to those I love,
    A Legacy To Dream.   *Paul Tsika*

Principle Two
Rooted in Community

It is vital to success to have roots that connect us in community!

    Two are better than one, because they have a good return for their work.1
    Though one may be overpowered, two can defend themselves. A cord of three strands is not quickly broken.2

If Sequoiadendron gigantean could talk, the second point in his famous lecture on how to have SEQUOIA SIZE SUCCESS would be: "Spread out with roots that bring you into inter-connected relationships with like-minded persons, who will provide mutual assistance and support".

We learned earlier in the amazing facts about Sequoias that they have remarkably shallow roots. There are estimates that suggest that 95% of these trees have roots no deeper than 3 feet! Despite their shallow roots, sequoias are resistant to toppling because their roots spread out over large areas, sometimes up to half an acre! Also they grow in groves with other sequoia with which they intertwine their root systems, thus providing mutual support for each other.

Spread out with roots that bring you into inter-connected relationships with like-minded persons who will provide mutual assistance and support.

As a result of community interdependence, what was a weakness is transformed into strength. The Sequoias live a long life, grow tall and do not fall because of the mutual support that comes from the deep-rooted togetherness of roots that are intertwined. The roots of the trees weave a foundational network at "root" level that strengthens one by being "all for one and one for all." Thus, having shallow roots (an apparent weakness) is changed into strength by being woven together by time, growth, the struggles of droughts and earthquakes, as well as raging fires.

Common unity is the key to community.

The simple truth is for one tree to fall, they would all have to fall. What do you think an organization could accomplish if that were our common attitude? That no matter what we go through, in order for one to fall or fail we would all have to fall. The psalmist talks of that kind of unity. He says, *"How good and pleasant it is for brethren to dwell (live, work, play) together in unity—for there the Lord commanded the blessing, even life forevermore."* [3] That's where the great life is.

In working with World Wide Dream Builders, I have seen close up the power this kind of unity brings. At one of the functions where I was speaking there was a lot of talk about community. When I simply said the word it broke into two words almost automatically: *Comm and Unity.* Maybe I'm just too simple, but it seems to me that *common unity* is the key to community. So with that in mind here is a great acrostic for community using the word *Together*.

T – Team work (A sense of belonging)
O – Oneness in responsibilities (A sense of bonding)
G – Giving and forgiving (A sharing of burdens)
E – Edification (A sharing of blessings)
T – Teaching (A setting forth of basic beliefs)
H – Holding yourself accountable
     (A sense of body life)
E – Evangelism (A sharing of beliefs)
R – Reproduction (Duplicating what we believe)

Whether it is a family, a church, a business or a nation, togetherness, partnership and fellowship form strong roots by networking people into genuine community. Community has been defined as a unified people who possess a common way, embrace a common truth and celebrate a common life.

Our English word "Fellowship" has an interesting etymology. It comes from the Anglo-Saxon *fee--lowship*. Fee means cow, which was the form that wealth took in medieval England. Neighbors put their cows together, breaking down the fence between them to show trust in each other, creating *fee-low-ship* through their joint partnership or cow-account.

> *Community has been defined as a unified people who possess a common way, embrace a common truth and celebrate a common life.*

In any good *fee-lowship* or partnership, the partners share equally in both the privileges and responsibilities, the assets and liabilities, and the blessings and burdens.

No person or organization can be truly successful without networking together in community. Americans pride ourselves in being ruggedly individualistic and rebelliously independent – after all, we have our own Declaration of Independence!

Realistically, however, this nation became great by interdependence and not independence. My wife loves to look through card shops for those unusual cards with hilarious captions. Often I have lost her in some mall only to find her held captive at a Hallmark shop laughing herself into hysterics. The upside of this is two fold. First, it puts her in a really great mood for the rest of the day. Proverbs says, "A merry heart does good like a medicine." Secondly, it gives me some really great material. The only downside is that when I find her, I have to read every card she thought funny. Her favorite are "Far Side" cards. When I think of independence, one card always comes to mind. On the card, there is a field filled with white sheep all grazing contently. Right in the middle is one sheep standing on his hind legs, with his front legs stretched out as far as possible. At the top of his lungs, he's screaming, *"I've Got To Be Me!"*

> *No person or organization can be truly successful without networking together in community.*

Independence is the tendency to try and make it on my own without community. This leads to rugged individualism. **Dependence**, on the other hand, leads to unhealthy relationships in which one becomes either a predator – aggressively using people, or a parasite, passively sucking the life out of people to further my goals or get my needs met. **Interdependence** is the practicing of mutual integration, fellowship and partnership with each other so that we order our lives by the context of the whole and not the limitation of the part.

The intertwining of our roots, like the sequoias, enables a family, a church, or an organization to become a community that is strengthened as we determine to be stepping-stones to the success of others, rather than stumbling-blocks! The interdependence of community is further strengthened

Real community changes the "I" and "me" to "we" and "us".

when we are determined to develop healthy relationships rather than demanding personal rights.

A synonym for interdependence is functioning as a TEAM. John Maxwell described the results of functioning as a TEAM by the acrostic: **T**ogether **E**veryone **A**ccomplishes **M**ore!

Kay Kuzma, in commenting on the strength of teamwork writes: *"The most important trait in strong, happy teams is commitment. Commitment to the team—putting the team first—and commitment to each individual on the team in helping him or her become everything he or she can be....With commitment comes the desire to help team members reach their potential. A winning attitude is 'I'll forgo my own immediate gratification to help a team member succeed, because I know the personal joy that I experience when I help another team member.'"*

Real community changes the "I" and "me" to "we" and "us". This produces more cooperation than competition. We begin to get a little horse sense. After reading the following poem, you'll better understand what I mean.

When days are hot and flies are thick,
Use horse sense – cooperate.
This is a truth all horses know;
They learned it many centuries ago.
One tail on duty at the rear
Can't reach that fly behind the ear.
But two tails when arranged with proper craft
Can do the job, both fore and aft!

How do we intertwine and interlock ourselves in solidarity – in community interdependence – so that we can help each other achieve our maximum potential?

1.) **By Being Real With One Another** – relating with other people doesn't occur in the dark but in the light. One of the reasons there is so little real community interdependence or "root-tangling" is because we try and use darkness to hide our hurts, faults, flaws, fears and failures.

> *The truth is you can't be healed and freed of what you fail to face and surrender.*

The Message says, *"...Make this your common practice: Confess your faults to each other and pray for each other so that you can live together whole and healed."* [4]

2.) By Building Relationships that are Healthy – *"From whom the whole body, joined and knit together by what every joint supplies, according to the effective working by which every part does its share, causes growth of the body for the edifying of itself in love."* [5]

"I want us to help each other with the faith we have. Your faith helping me, and my faith will help you." [6]

Truly Healthy Relationships are Built on Sharing Common Life and Love with Each Other! There is a prayer that seems to cross all culture barriers. A prayer for unity and a prayer when prayed that forces us to pray in community. *"OUR Father which art in Heaven. Hallowed be Thy Name. Thy Kingdom come. Thy Will be done in Earth, as it is in Heaven. Give US this day OUR daily bread. And forgive US OUR debts, as WE forgive OUR debtors. And lead US not into temptation, but deliver US from evil; for Thine is the Kingdom, and the Power, and the Glory, forever, Amen."*

> *I want to reiterate that no human being can meet all our needs.*

I want to reiterate that no human being can meet all our needs. The eros *(self-preferential type love)* hook of wanting to get my needs met by another person other than God will make me either a predator *(aggressive)*, running to death and killing all relationships or a parasite *(passive)*, sucking the life out of others and thus killing relationships! There is to be a mutual and reciprocal giving and receiving in the Community of Faith. There are more than fifty commands in the New Testament in which we are commanded to certain ministries and duties to "one another" and "each other."

3.) **By Being Supportive of Each Other** — *"Bear one another's burdens, and so fulfill the law of Christ."* [7]

What works in the Church will also work in other communities as well. Standing together in community requires that we should always seek to compassionately restore the dislocated or hurting member. [8] We are to do this authoritatively without excusing the failure, accurately without exaggerating the failure and affectionately by extending forgiveness towards the one who has failed.

A vital part of standing together in community is seeking to jointly relieve the heavy-laden member. In order to do this we must approach them with an attitude of forbearance – *"Bear with each other and forgive whatever grievances you may have against one another. Forgive as the Lord forgave you."* [9] We must do it freely without expecting returned favors. Often times this requires us to provide a helping hand, an understanding heart, a present body and sometime a shut mouth. There

> *There are times when silence is yellow and other times when it's golden!*

are times when silence is yellow and other times when it's golden! Our mutual assistance to those in the same "grove" with us must be approached humbly in a spirit of equality. We are cautioned to be on guard against superior feelings in which I feel better than you because I'm not going through your challenge. On the other hand, feeling inferior can cause us to reject any attempts at burden-bearing based on the false perception that we think that you think you're better than us and we resent it.

Growing together for success requires us to be merciful towards one another... *"Therefore be merciful, just as your Father also is merciful"*[10]; to be honest with one another; to be humble around each other; to be courteous in respect to our differences; to be trustworthy

> *Growing together for success requires us to be merciful towards one another.*

with regards to confidentiality; and to be consistent in regards to watching out for one another.

The Independent Grocers Association demonstrates the indispensableness of standing together in their IGA anthem:

When we stand together, we can stand the test.
Standing together, we stand out from the rest.
When we stand together, when we all join in.
When we stand together, we stand to win.
As we all look toward the future, we can dream of what can be.
For we have the strength to realize the future that we see.
If we always give our very best and we always lead the way,
We can stand for all the best in life and stand for IGA!
When we stand together, we can stand the test.

United we stand, divided we fall!

There is an admonishment from scripture for every organization that understands the power of unity and strives to maintain it.

When there is no unity,
Strife comes in.
Then division.
Then faith quits working.
And when faith quits working,
Sickness comes in,
Financial disaster appears,
Spiritual stagnation sets in,
And everything becomes a mess.
Simply because somebody
thought more highly of himself
than he should have. [11]

Remember to have SEQUOIA-SIZE SUCCESS we must be like the Sequoia with our lives so interwoven that we become interdependent, living and growing together.

Principle Three
Rooted in Integrity

Stand straight and tall in integrity or you will eventually fall!

"The man of integrity walks securely, but he who takes crooked paths will be found out." [1]

"The integrity of the upright guides them, but the unfaithful are destroyed by their duplicity." [2]

If Sequoiadendron gigantean were a talking tree, the third point in his famous lecture on how to have SEQUOIA-SIZE SUCCESS would be: *"Integrity is not rooted in public or professional life, but in your personal life!"*

The tallest standing giant sequoia is 311 feet tall. It could have never reached such towering heights by growing crooked or by being rotten on the inside. This principle of success focuses on integrity, without which standing tall is only the temporary state prior to a disastrous fall.

Integrity is not rooted in public or professional life, but in your personal life!

Dr. O.S. Hawkins insight-fully declares, "Integrity is rooted in your private life, reflected in your personal life, reinforced in your professional life and revealed in your public life."

True success is always built on the foundation of integrity. God's design for us is to build integrity into our hearts. So much of the time we are more concerned about building our image. Integrity is defined as "the state of being complete, unified." The integrity that God builds and approves has nothing to do with wealth, education, brilliance of mind, outward appearance or social standing. It is all about the deep, inner core of godly character. When I have integrity, my words and my deeds match up. I am who I am, no matter where I am or who I am with. Image is what people think we are. Integrity is what we really are.

There are three people in every one of us:
   #1—The one we think we are
   #2—The one others think we are
   #3—The one God knows we are

Now if you were to take a wild guess, which person carries the weight of integrity? I primarily minister to men and women in leadership capacity. And if there is one thing I am convinced of without reservation, it's this: you can lead without integrity (character), but integrity (character) is what makes a leader worth following.

Humorist Will Rogers understood the meaning of integrity when he said, "So live that you would not mind selling your pet parrot to the town gossip."

Integrity is our fundamental core value, our inner reality.

Integrity comes from the word "integer," meaning whole. In other words, the real meaning of integrity is wholeness of character. It's thinking and doing the right thing when no one is looking. It requires consistency, honesty and

> *You can lead without integrity, but integrity is what makes a leader worth following.*

courage to ensure our actions are aligned with what we know is right. It's doing the right thing as a matter of habit — not just some of the time, but all the time in our professional and personal lives.

Chuck Swindoll writes: "Real integrity stays in place whether the test is prosperity or adversity." Billy Graham writes, "Integrity is the glue that holds our way of life together." Dennis Waitley, "You must consider the bottom line, but make it Integrity before profits."

Two old ladies were walking around a somewhat over-crowded English country churchyard and came upon a tomb-stone whose inscription read: "Here lies John Smith, a politician and an honest man." "Good heavens," said one of the ladies, "Isn't it awful that they had to put two people in the same grave!"

On a job application one question read, "Have you ever been arrested?" The guy applying for the job printed the word "no" in the space. The next question was a follow-up to the first. It asked, "Why?" Not realizing he didn't have to answer this part, the honest and naïve applicant wrote, "I guess it's because I never got caught!"

Groucho Marx said, "The secret of life is honesty and fair dealing. If you can fake that, you got it made."

The truth is all of life is lived from the inside out. You can't fake integrity. At the very center of your personality lay your values about yourself and life in general. These values determine the kind of person you really are. What you stand for, and what you won't stand for, tells you and the world the kind of person you have become. Integrity is expressed in terms of constancy and consistency, of honesty and truthfulness.

David Sweet explains that *"Promise Keepers of Canada used the definition of integrity as being equal strength throughout the whole. Strength is developed and so is integrity. As we exercise our muscles they grow and we find we are able to handle more and respond to physical duress more effectively. As we exercise keeping our word and the dedication to keeping it, we will grow in character and integrity."*

Strength is developed and so is integrity.

In 1826, one of the world's greatest financial organizations, Hearst and Robinson of Great Britain filed bankruptcy. During the trial, each of the principals was asked, "Do you admit to your indebtedness and claim bankruptcy?" Each one replied yes but one, Sir Walter Scott. Scott raised his right hand and said, "I admit my debt, but this right hand and I promise that we will not rest until our debt is fully paid." Within 10 years, the majority of those men were either destitute or had committed suicide. But as for Sir Walter Scott, well—with that right hand, he wrote 49 of The Waverly

Novels, including such classics as *Ivanhoe* and *Rob Roy*. With the proceeds of these novels, he fully discharged his debt and made another fortune. What made the difference: right character that produced a right commitment that manifested integrity.

> *Integrity is more valuable than riches.*

What does the Bible have to say about integrity?

1. Integrity means treating people fairly and honestly. (Leviticus 19:35-36, Deut 25:15, Proverbs 16:11-13)
2. Integrity is giving your word and keeping it. (Exodus 8:28-32)
3. Integrity will protect you. In Psalm 25, David prays that integrity and uprightness will protect him. How can it? (Psalm 25:21, Proverbs 2:7-8, 10:9, 11:3, 13:6)
4. Integrity is more valuable than riches. (Proverbs 28:6)
5. The Lord will test and judge your integrity. (1 Chronicles 29:17, Psalm 7:8)
6. The Lord hates lies and lack of integrity. (Zechariah 8:16-17)
7. It may be a battle to maintain your integrity. (Job 2:3, 2:9, Proverbs 29:10)
8. Your character can be corrupted by bad company. (1 Corinthians 15:33)
9. Integrity will be rewarded. (1 Kings 9:4-5, Nehemiah 7:2, Psalm 41:11-12)
10. Your integrity should set an example. (Titus 2:7)

Another classic illustration of integrity is Eric Liddell, whose life inspired the movie, *Chariots of Fire*.

Eric was a man who demonstrated the reality of integrity by refusing to compromise his convictions concerning the Sabbath. He refused to run in the Olympics on Sunday in his best event, nevertheless he entered a different race and won a gold medal in the 1924 Olympics. Eric Liddell was called to be a missionary to China and became a teacher at the Anglo-Chinese College in Tientsin. After teaching for some time, he went into the interior and traveled from village to village on foot and by bicycle—spreading the gospel over hundreds of thousands of miles.

After the Japanese invasion of China in World War II, Liddell was branded, along with many others of Western heritage, as an "enemy national," and in 1943 he was confined in a prison camp 150 by 200 yards with a thousand other so-called nationalist enemies. While there he had an impact on the prison camp—he organized athletic events, conducted worship services, preached the gospel (to which many responded in faith), counseled people, and comforted the sick and the dying.

His determined influence is reflected in the writings of David Michell who was a child in the camp during that time. Michell wrote: "None of us will ever forget this man who was totally committed to putting God first, a man whose humble life combined muscular Christianity with radiant godliness." (Eric Liddell, *The Disciplines of the Christian Life*, 18). In 1945 Eric Liddell died of a brain tumor in that prison camp.

Liddell's story gives insight into the meaning of integrity. He articulated that integrity in a Christian manual that gives four tests of the moral law by which we are to measure ourselves:

1. **"Am I truthful?** Are there any conditions under which I will tell a lie? Can I be depended on to tell the truth no matter what the cost?"

2. **"Am I honest?** Can I be trusted in money matters? How about at work, when no one is looking? With other people's reputations? With myself—or do I rationalize and become defensive?"

3. **"Am I pure:** In my habits? In my thought life? In my motives? In my relations with the opposite sex?"

4. **"Am I selfish:** In the demands I make on my family, spouse, or associates? Am I badly balanced, full of moods— cold today and warm tomorrow? Do I indulge in nerves that spoil my happiness and that of those around me? Am I unrestrained in my

> *Integrity demands that there be no twilight zone-- something is either right or it is wrong; black or it is white.*

pleasures, the kind I enjoy without considering the effect...to take reasonable rest and exercise? Am I unrestrained in small self-indulgences, letting myself become the slave of habits, however harmless they may appear to me? Let us put ourselves before ourselves and look at ourselves." (Liddell, *The Disciplines of the Christian Life*, 29-30)."

From an unknown author come these truths concerning integrity:

> *"It cannot be bought and it cannot be measured in money. It is a prerequisite in determining the fiber and character of an individual and an organization. Integrity demands that there be no twilight zone-- something is either right or it is wrong; black or it is white. Principles may be inborn ethics or, sometimes, mandated. But integrity requires scourging moral courage, magnetized by fervor for an ideal. The complete person is a union of unswerving integrity, pulsating energy, and rugged determination--and the greatest of these is integrity."*

To reflect integrity is to invest trust. To possess integrity is to command respect. Integrity is found in simple issues and those complex. Its presence is critical. It demands total loyalty, a commitment to cause, a dedication to mission and unflagging determination.

Honesty isn't the best policy. It is the only policy.

Morals, Ethics, Standards, and Integrity... from these flow a torrent of values. Deeds, not words. It is clear that what you do overshadows what you are speaking with deafening impact. Honesty isn't the best policy; it is the only policy. For an organization, integrity isn't a sometimes thing; it is everything. As one man said, "It's never right to do wrong and never wrong to do right."

President Abraham Lincoln prayed, "God grant that men of principle shall be the principal men."

Always remember that success requires growing straight and tall with integrity of heart. King David of old reminds us that God is pleased with integrity: *"I know, my God, that you test the heart and are pleased with integrity."* [3]

The Apostle Paul writes to his disciple Titus and challenges him to be an exemplary leader by being a person of integrity: *"In everything set them an example by doing what is good. In your teaching show integrity, seriousness and soundness of speech that cannot be condemned, so that those who oppose you may be ashamed because they have nothing bad to say about us."*[4]

Listed below are a few proverbs that would serve us well to memorize and live.

Proverbs 10:2 *"Ill gotten gain gets you nowhere, an honest life is immortal."*

Proverbs 11:1 *"God hates cheating in the marketplace; he loves it when business is aboveboard."*

Proverbs 11:20 *"God can't stand deceivers, but oh how he relishes integrity."*

Proverbs 19:1 *"Better to be poor and honest than a rich person no one can trust."*

Proverbs 20:10 *"Switching price tags and padding the expense account are two things God hates."*

Proverbs 20:23 *"God hates cheating in the marketplace; rigged scales are an outrage."*

Proverbs 21:3 *"Clean living before God and justice with our neighbors mean far more to God than religious performance."*

Principle Four
Thrive in the Fire

Develop the ability to thrive in the fires of life and not just survive!

When you walk through the fire, you shall not be burned, Nor shall the flame scorch you.[1]

For he will be like a tree planted by the water, That extends its roots by a stream And will not fear when the heat comes; But its leaves will be green, And it will not be anxious in a year of drought Nor cease to yield fruit.[2]

Beloved, do not think it strange concerning the fiery trial which is to try you, as though some strange thing happened to you.[3]

One of the reasons for the success of the sequoia tree is its unusually thick bark, which is fire-resistant. Unlike most tree barks, the bark has no resin in it, so it doesn't burn very well. In addition, the bark is very thick—sometimes more than two feet at the base—and this insulates the tree and protects it. Actually the sequoias depend on fires to thin out the firs and pines around them that would be competitors for the water and nutrients. Without the fires that burn the brush, the sequoias would eventually choke to death. Likewise, giant sequoia seeds do well in a fire-mineralized soil, and in fact, need the heat of the fire to cause the release of their seeds from the cones in the most prolific numbers after the fire.

Fire is also essential for the propagation of the sequoias. The heat of the fire opens their cones and allows the seeds to emerge. It also burns off the undergrowth and sterilizes the ground, creating a nice little nursery for the seeds. Without the competition from the other plants and trees, the young sequoias have a chance to take root and flourish.

A typical fire in a sequoia forest leaves no marks on the giant trees! Their branches begin at a height of 100 feet, so there is no chance for the fire to reach them. The trees lack the flammable resin typical of other trees, which makes them fireproof if the fire moves fast enough through the under-brush. However, if the fire is hot enough it will burn into the trunk of one of these giants. The fire will leave a charred wound, but the tree begins immediately to repair the damage. In the growing season following the fire, the tree will grow slabs of wood thicker than the bark on the rest of the tree in order to cover the burned portion. This unique ability of the redwood/sequoia tree to withstand fire, disease and insect attack accounts for their long life span.

God's design for us is not to just try to survive the fiery trails of life but to thrive because of them! When the firestorms assault many people or their businesses, they develop the attitude of a store owner who posted the follow-ing notice in the window of his coat store in Nottingham, England: "We have been established for over 100 years and have been pleasing and displeasing customers ever since. We have made money and lost money, suffered the effects of coal nationalization, coal rationing, government control, and bad payers. We have been cussed and discussed, messed about, lied to, held up, robbed, and swindled. The only reason we stay in business is to see what happens next."

The store owner knew that life was full of difficulties. But he was determined to survive, even if only to hope for the best and "see what happens next." God is not in to our just surviving but in to our thriving in the hardest and hottest of times.

God's design for us is not to just try to survive the fiery trials of life but to thrive because of them!

In England in 1567, a church building was erected and this plaque was attached to it: *"In the midst of the worst of times when all things in the kingdom were profaned and defiled, this church was built to do the best of things in the worst of times."* That church building and the church that meets in it still stand today after all these many years.

When the firestorms of life rage around us, how can we still do the best of things in the worst of times? How do we learn to profit from the painful, scorching experiences that come our way in life and in business?

1.) One of the key factors is that when we find ourselves in the midst of one of life's firestorms, we must ask the right questions.

We must avoid those "why me"-type questions shot up to

God—they almost always come back blank—but in the midst of the fire ask:

- Is this fiery storm due to satanic opposition? If so, what the enemy means for evil—God means for good.
- Is this a fiery storm that I am in due to the foolishness of the expert opinions of those in authority over me so that I had no choice but to don my fire-retardant suit and get ready for the heat to be turned up? If so I will stand in the midst of the fiery trial and declare that this fire, although painful, will only serve to burn away all that would choke the life out of me and rob me of the nourishment of God's grace and hinder me from achieving my destiny.
- Is this fiery storm my fault because of my disobedience to the revealed will of God for my life or is it due to foolish violations of basic business principles? If so, I need to cry out in repentance to God for mercy and plan on being like the Phoenix rising out of the ashes to a new tomorrow.
- Is this a fiery storm that I've encountered due to my obediently following the will of God for my life? If so, He intends for me to rise up and walk through it with Him so that I become more fruitful.

By the way, don't ever answer the "How are you doing" question by saying, "Well, pretty good under the circumstances!" Come out from under there. We are to live in the grace of God and not under life's circumstances!

2.) **A second principle of thriving, instead of just surviving in the firestorms of life is learning how to stay in season with God even when you don't know the reason!**

In nature, in order for fruit trees to produce and mature their fruit, the summer heat is turned on. The heat causes the fruit to pop out and begin to grow. The most rapid of changes occur in the "hot" seasons of life. Change is the only thing that brings growth. However, the truth is that we don't usually change because we see the light, but because we feel the heat. We are like a tea bag, not worth much until we've been through some hot water!

Peter reminded us not to *"think it strange concerning the fiery trial which is to try you, as though some strange thing happened unto you."* If our roots are right we never have to fear the heat — *"For he will be like a tree planted by the water, that extends its roots by a stream; and will not fear when the heat comes; but its leaves will be green, and it will not be anxious in a year of drought, nor cease to yield fruit."* [4]

> *Change is the only thing that brings growth.*

3.) **A third principle of fire-resistant living is learning to stand in submission to God even when we don't understand!**

We are to cooperate with our Heavenly Father by abiding in and obeying Him. *"Now no chastening for the present seems to be joyous, but grievous: nevertheless afterward it yields the peaceable fruit of righteousness unto them which are exercised thereby."* [5]

All the blessings, the beatings, the bleedings, the break-ings, the bakings of God's dealings with us are not designed to punish us but to prosper us; not to make us hurt, but to make us ready for the harvest!

Don't be a quitter or a complainer - stand when you don't understand!

We must not quit on God or quarrel with His dealings in our lives. We must not be like the man who joined a monastery where the monks were allowed to speak only two words every seven years. After seven years he met with the bishop who asked, "Well, what are your two words?" He said, "Food's bad." Then he went back to spend another seven years in total silence. After the next seven years were up, he appeared before the same bishop who asked , "What are your two words now?" "Bed's hard!" replied the man. He went back and spent another seven years in silence after which he went before the bishop for the third and final time. "Well, what are your two words now?" "I QUIT!" screamed the man. "I'm not surprised," said the bishop, "all you've done since you've been here is complain!" Don't be a quitter or a complainer — stand when you don't understand! God promises us, *"And let us not be weary in well doing: for in due season we shall reap, if we faint not."* [6]

Thomas Edison invented the microphone, the phono-graph, the incandescent light, the storage battery, talking movies, and more than 1000 other things. In December of 1914, he had worked for 10 years on a storage battery. This had greatly strained his finances. This particular evening spontaneous combustion had broken out in the film room. Within minutes all the packing compounds, celluloid for records and film, and other flammable goods were in flames. Fire companies from eight surrounding towns arrived, but the heat was so intense and the water pressure so low that the attempt to douse the flames was futile. Everything was destroyed. Edison was 67 years of age.

With all his assets going up in a whoosh (although the damage exceeded two million dollars, the buildings were only insured for $238,000 because they were made of concrete and thought to be fireproof), would his spirit be broken?

The inventor's 24-year old son, Charles, searched frantically for his father. He finally found him, calmly watching the fire, his face glowing in the reflection, his white hair blowing in the wind. "My heart ached for him," said Charles. "He was 67—no longer a young man—and everything was going up in flames. When he saw me, he shouted, 'Charles, where's your mother?' When I told him I didn't know, he said, 'Find her. Bring her here. She will never see anything like this as long as she lives.'"

The next morning, Edison looked at the ruins and said, "There is great value in disaster. All our mistakes are burned up. Thank God we can start anew." Three weeks after the fire, Edison managed to

> *There is great value in disaster: All our mistakes are burned up.*

deliver the first phonograph! This is the sequoia principle of thriving and not just surviving the firestorms of life!

4.) Another key to thriving in the firestorms that come raging into our lives is to feed our enthusiasm with faith and maintain a sense of humor. Enthusiasm must be fed with faith or it will flame out.

Faith in God and His promises will keep your vision clear and big and your vitality fresh and fun! John Maxwell said, "I often meet people who are drowning in life's problems. Yet, it really isn't their problems that are weighing them down; it's their lack of vision. A big vision will help you overcome any problem, but a small vision or no vision at all will cause the smallest of problems to trip you up and keep you from becoming what you should be."

Winston Churchill said, "Success is going from failure to failure without loss of enthusiasm!"

Mike Mason was right when he said, "Develop a sense of humor. It will help you overlook the unattractive, tolerate the unpleasant, handle the unexpected, and smile through the unbearable." If you can laugh at it, you can live with it. Smiling and laughing is a lot like changing a baby's diaper — it solves a problem, and makes things smell a lot better for a while! But I say, "You may have to eat a lot of crow in this life, but if you'll eat it while it's hot, it won't taste too bad."

Almost everyone knows the story of Colonel Sanders, but it will assist you in maintaining a "thriver" and not just a "survivor" mentality, if you will rehearse his story when the firestorms of life seem to burn up all efforts at success.

"A 63-year-old man named Harlan had every excuse in the world to play the role of a victim—but chose to become a victor instead! At one time Harlan owned a restaurant-motel-service station business he'd built up over the years. He was offered nearly $200,000 cash for the business, but turned down the offer

Success is going from failure to failure without loss of enthusiasm!

because he wasn't quite ready to retire yet. Two years later the state built a new superhighway bypassing his business. Within a year Harlan lost everything.

Here he was, 65 years old, flat broke, and no income other than a small monthly Social Security check to live on. The only thing he knew how to do well was cook chicken. Maybe he could sell that knowledge to someone else. So he kissed his wife goodbye, loaded up his battered old car with a pressure cooker and his special recipe, and set out to sell his idea to the world.

It was tough going, and he often slept in his car because there wasn't enough money for a hotel room. Restaurant after restaurant turned him down. Harlan suffered 100, 200, even 300 rejections before he found someone to believe in his dream. A few years later he opened the first of what would become thousands of successful restaurants located around the world. The man was Harlan Sanders. Most likely you know him better by his more recognizable name - Colonel Sanders, the legend behind Kentucky Fried Chicken."

An old hymn bolsters our faith in God's ability to guide, provide and prosper us through the firestorms that rage in and around our lives:

Fear not, I am with thee - O be not dismayed,
For I am thy God, I will still give thee aid;
I'll strengthen thee, help thee, and cause thee to stand,
Upheld by My righteous, omnipotent hand.
When thru fiery trials thy pathway shall lie,
My grace, all sufficient, shall be thy supply;
The flame shall not hurt thee- I only design
Thy dross to consume and thy gold to refine.

What is the Secret to Abounding in Adversity?

(a)   We must Foresee our Afflictions Constructively.

(b)   We must Focus our Attention Correctly.

(c)   We must Finish our Assignment Completely.

(d)   We must Form our Attitudes Correctly.

(e)   We must Face our Adversaries Confidently.

Principle Five
Pest Attacks

Do not let the personal attacks of pests "bug" you to death!

Another factor of the sequoia tree that enables it to have sequoia size success is its ability to fight off insects that would literally "bug it" to death. The sequoia is able to do this because it contains a natural wood preservative and is very resistant to disease. It has the ability to ward off disease or insects. In fact, it has been said that "no known disease will kill a mature redwood."

No one knows how long a redwood/sequoia can live. "Most of the Sierra trees die of disease, fungi, etc." John Muir wrote, "but nothing hurts the Big Tree, i.e., the sequoia. Barring accidents, it seems to be immortal." Muir was partially right. Chemicals in the wood and bark provide resistance to insects and fungi.

Many people who claim they don't let little things bug them have never slept in a room with a mosquito. More than often, little things in life seem to bother us more than the big things. A lone mosquito buzzing around your bedroom at night can easily become the focus of all your attention and keep you awake.

The Charlie Brown cartoon character, Lucy, speaking to Snoopy says, "There are times when you really bug me, but I must admit there are also times when I feel like giving you a hug." Snoopy replied, "That's the way I am, huggable and buggable!" Unfortunately, it seems that most of us are more buggable than huggable!

> *Many people who claim they don't let little things bug them have never slept in a room with a mosquito.*

How do we prevent the pestering, potentially destructive conflicts and attacks that inevitably come our way in life, in business and in church, from "bugging" us to death? How do we handle those persons who are like "boring beetles" that try to get under our skin and eat away our vitality?

One of the first principles of conflict management and conflict resolution is to **Seek Clarity**. By this we mean when facing any conflict in life we should seek to clarify the issues. We need to separate the people from the problem and focus on facts and not on personalities. We must learn to be gentle with people while at the same time being hard on the problem. This requires establishing clear lines of communication. We must develop the ability to use a problem solving, rather than a win-lose approach. All the while we keep in mind that the primary problem is usually secondary (normally it was really something else).

Most of the attacks on the sequoia tree come from *wood boring beetles*. Likewise, the most powerful and destructive insect for us humans is what I call "Word Boring Beetles."

These "bugger" type creatures use the mouths of both enemies and friends (and our own mouth as well) to get under
our skin. They carry out their attacks in a variety of ways.
They may attack using name-calling, stereotyping or pigeon-
holing terms. They may attempt to attach value-laden, dis-
crediting or shameful labels on our character. Some of those
labels read: *"hypocrite," "trouble-maker," "sower of doubt,"*
"brown-noser," "back-stabber," etc. An attack may cast doubt
on our intelligence, integrity, sanity, judgment, morality
and spirituality. Some word-borers attack by pointing out
how you or your actions have adversely affected them: i.e.
caused them to be disappointed, embarrassed, angry,
ashamed, pained or put them in harm's way.

Personal attacks may take the form of insult, ridiculing,
belittling, mocking, taunting, shaming, scorning or
battering.

Brooks Faulkner, Pastoral Ministry Specialist at LifeWay
Christian Resources, lists nine of what I would point out as
potentially destructive "bugger" type persons:

The Sherman tank will run right over you.
The star performer feels entitled to your preferential
    treatment.
The megaphone will talk your ear off.
The bubble buster deflates everyone's enthusiasm.
The volcano has a temper like Mt. St. Helens.
The crybaby is a chronic complainer.
The nitpicker is an unpleasable perfectionist.
The backbiter is a master of calculated rumor.
The space cadet is on a different wavelength.

Word-borers may attack what you **ARE** by pointing out some alleged, undesirable character flaw, such as being unwilling, rebellious, difficult, doubtful, vain, deceived, bitter, unhappy, troubled and miserable. They may attack you because of what you **ARE NOT** -- not for real, not trustworthy, properly submissive, humble, etc.

These little bugs may attack with the intent to shame you. This type of attack may be directed towards some things you **HAVE**, such as the wrong reasons, ulterior motives, wrong spirit, bad attitude, doubt, unbelief, because you **DON'T HAVE** enough contacts in high places, enthusiasm for the business, faith, willingness, submission, etc. Attacks are sometimes accusations of some selfish things you allegedly **WANT**, such as; to be noticed, to take control, to get attention, to "get all you can and can all you get, while sitting on the lid and poisoning all the rest". There may be accusations that you **DON'T WANT** to be a team player, to be understanding or to really help others reach their goals.

Some attacks are engineered so you will feel ashamed about things you **DO** or **DID**. Examples of these are cause trouble or strife, mistakes or failures you made, poor judgments you made, etc.

Because all of us have a desperate need to feel important to someone that really matters, to feel valuable, loved, admired, accepted, approved, and affirmed in life, we longingly seek to have our needs met. However, due to our inheritance of a sin principle and our personal involvement in sin, we tend to allow *word bugs* to lay the eggs of inferiority, inadequacy, guilt, rejection, unworthiness and insecurity in our minds. These hatch into the guard bugs that cause us to be protective of our emotional turf, withdrawn, feeling unloved, unaccepted and making it very hard to show and give love. This offspring produces protective nests of personal inferiority, spiritual insecurity and relational incompatibility. The solution requires that we learn how to handle personal indignities and accept personal inequities.

All of us have a desperate need to feel important.

There are a host of other "bugging" tactics that the enemy uses to try to bore into our hearts and minds and eat away our vision and vitality. The Old Testament book of Nehemiah sets forth one of the most insightful revelations of enemy tactics found anywhere. Time and space constraints will limit us to giving only the outline and the reference. Taking time to read and develop each of these "bug tactics" could save you from getting bored to death! Are these great puns or what?

Enemy Strategy -- DERISION – Nehemiah 4:1-3 –Biblical Solution – We Must Have a Mind to Pray -- Nehemiah 4:4-5, 9

Enemy Strategy -- DISCOURAGEMENT -- Nehemiah 4:10 - Biblical Solution – We Must Have a Victory Orientation and a Vision of the Task -- Nehemiah 4:14

Enemy Strategy -- DANGER -- Nehemiah 4:11-- Biblical Solution – We Must have an Eye to Watch -- 4:13; a Mind to Work -- 4:6, 14-15; a Will to Fight -- 4:16

Enemy Strategy -- DISCORD -- Nehemiah 5:1 -- Biblical Solution – We Must Have a Sense of Stewardship versus Ownership

Enemy Strategy -- DEPLETION -- Nehemiah 5:3-5 -- Biblical Solution – We Must Have a Heart that's Generous instead of Greedy

Enemy Strategy -- DISTRACTION AND DEFAMATION -- Nehemiah 6:1-2, 6-8 -- Biblical Solution – We Must Have a Sense of Divine Destiny -- 6:3

Enemy Strategy -- DISMAY -- Nehemiah 6:9 -- Biblical Solution – We Must Have a Will to Finish Victoriously -- 6:15

Bob Sheffield, Pastoral Ministry Specialist at LifeWay Christian Resources, made the following observations about **Difficult People**:

1. *Everybody has one.*
2. *Everybody becomes one to someone.*
3. *We cannot change them but we can learn to relate.*
4. *We will not get along equally with everyone (some may not like us).*
5. *We should not expect everyone to agree with, like, or love us all the time.*
6. *We must manage our expectations of others and ourselves.*
7. *We give up too soon on some relationships.*
8. *We get along best when we mature spiritually and emotionally.*

A leader must demonstrate wisdom and exercise restraint in responding to personal attacks. Jesus gives the method that we are to use in handling relationships in general and personal attacks in particular: *"Behold, I send you out as sheep in the midst of wolves. Therefore be wise as serpents and harmless as doves."*[1] Resisting personal attacks requires the Shrewdness of the Serpent and the Guilelessness of the Dove!

> *A leader must demonstrate wisdom and exercise restraint in responding to personal attacks.*

Please note that Jesus didn't encourage us to be sneaky as a fox, or stubborn as a mule, or sloppy as a pig or grumpy as a bear. He said, *"Be wise as a serpent and harmless as a dove."* Sent out into the world of wolves, we sheep, in order to thrive and not just survive, must portray shrewdness like a snake and gentleness like a dove! What in the world do snakes and doves have in common? Very little! Yet, in getting outfitted for "bug-battle," we're required to be as they are in some respects. In other words, some traits of both are to be built into our lives. For example, we are to control our tongue, yet also to speak boldly. We're to be humble, yet confident. Our love is to be both tough and tender. Because we're prone by nature to be as serpents or doves, the tendency is to develop what comes natural and most comfortable and excuse the lack of the other by saying, "Well, that's just not my nature." This results in an imbalance in our character and causes us to go to extremes. The naturally serpent-type character would tend to be sneaky and snappy, striking out when touched. The dove-type personality would tend to be shy and sweet. They would tend to project a pseudo-sophistication that declares that "cultured" people avoid bold speech, confident declarations, intolerance of sin, and anything that might offend anyone.

The word translated "wise or shrewd," is the Greek word "phronimos." It is used 17 times in the New Testament and refers to practical wisdom, prudence, cleverness and discernment.

To use the wisdom of the serpent means basically three things: Having and deploying **(1) A perceptiveness in avoiding unhealthy contact and unnecessary conflict.** A snake is wise enough to try to avoid unnecessary contact that could lead to deadly conflict. **(2) A cleverness in catching our prey; (3) A timeliness in choosing the moment to act.** One rarely sees a snake chasing its prey or thrashing about trying to impress it. It chooses the right moment and then acts quickly and decisively.

Dr. Joe Sherrer shares seven principles that are characteristic of the person who is as wise as a serpent in conflict management and resolution:

1. Realize you cannot please everybody
Here Jesus deals with a group of difficult people by appealing to four witnesses of His authority: John the Baptist, His miracles, the Father, and the Scriptures. [2]

2. Refuse to play their game
The Pharisees tried to catch Jesus by pitting him against the government. He refused to play, *"But perceiving their malice, Jesus said, "Why are you testing Me, hypocrites? Show Me*

the coin used for the tax." So they brought Him a denarius. 'Whose image and inscription is this?' He asked them. Then He answered, "Render unto Caesar that which is Caesar's and unto God, that which is God's." [3]

3. Never retaliate. *"You have heard that it was said, An eye for an eye and a tooth for a tooth. On the contrary, if anyone slaps you on your right cheek, turn the other to him also." [4]*

4. Pray for them *"But I tell you, love your enemies and pray for those who persecute you, so that you may be sons of your Father in heaven. For He causes His sun to rise on the evil and the good, and sends rain on the righteous and the unrighteous."[5]*

5. Control your temper . *"From now on, then, we do not know anyone in a purely human way ... He has committed the message of reconciliation to us."[6]*

6. Be quick to forgive and even quicker to ask for forgiveness. *"For if you forgive people their wrongdoing, your heavenly Father will forgive you as well. But if you don't forgive people, your Father will not forgive your wrongdoing." [7]*

7. Remember that everything has God's fingerprints on it. *"If one wanted to take Him to court, he could not answer God once in a thousand [times]. God is wise and all-powerful. Who has opposed Him and come out unharmed? He removes mountains without their knowledge, overturning them in His anger."[8]*

Employing the innocence of the Dove means having and deploying three things as well:

1. *Uprightness of character* — The word in the KJV translated "harmless" is the Greek word akeraios, which means unmixed, i.e. (fig.) innocent, harmless, simple. Paul uses it, *"Everyone has heard about your obedience, so I am full of joy over you; but I want you to be wise about what is good, and innocent (akeraios) about what is evil."* [9]

God is large and in charge!

And again, *"that you may become blameless and harmless (akeraios) (pure NIV; innocent NASB), children of God without fault in the midst of a crooked and perverse generation, among whom you shine as lights in the world,"* [10]

2. *Gentleness in conduct* — *"But the wisdom that is from above is first pure, then peaceable, gentle (epieikes, ep-ee-i-kace -- appropriate, i.e. by implication,) mild, gentle, moderation, patient), and easy to be entreated, full of mercy and good fruits, without partiality, and without hypocrisy."* [11] Paul writes, *"to speak evil of no one, to be peaceable, gentle, showing all humility to all men."* [12] *"And a servant of the Lord must not quarrel but be gentle to all, able to teach, patient."* [13]

3. *Faithfulness to commitments* — A classic example is the Old Testament story of Nathan the prophet is confronting King David with his sin.[14] He confronted him in such a manner as to gently give him the rope and then allow him to hang himself with it.

If we are going to have sequoia-size success in life, we must learn what options are available to us when wrongs are committed against us and choose the right one. I borrow heavily from my dear friend Herb Hodges at this point as he states that, "There are three levels of revenge which may be practiced to avenge yourself against personal wrongs. *One is the level of unlimited revenge.* By this standard, if you strike me, I may kill you in reaction. *A second level is limited revenge.* By this standard, if you wrong me, I am entitled to a reprisal against you that is equal in kind and degree to the wrong you have done to me. This is the Old Testament standard of revenge, often called *The Law of Retaliation.* This standard is stated in Exodus.[15] This option of retaliation is expressed in our society in a popular couplet, 'Tit for tat, Butter for fat, You kill my dog, I'll kill your cat.' *The third level is God's way of revenge which was taught by Jesus: 'Ye have heard that it hath been said, An eye for an eye, and a tooth for a tooth... But I say unto you, don't give into evil: but whosoever shall smite thee on thy right cheek, turn to him the other also.'"* [16]

Listen closely and you can hear your old nature, the flesh, arguing with these principles. "These are not practical in our sinful, violent world. Why, you have got to look out for number one! You must do it unto others before they do it unto you. Why, if you approached life this way everybody would run over you and take advantage of you. We are not to be like doormats are we? I don't get mad, I get even!"

But the truth is, that though acts of revenge may provide temporary satisfaction, they soon develop into a bitter poison that envelops a person's life and poisons everything that they are, do and say. Eventually they withdraw into their own little world, refusing to associate with anyone, never having a good word for anyone, always being critical, skeptical, distrustful and blaming other people for the situations in which they find themselves. Slowly they poison all meaningful relationships in life and poison themselves in the process. The unconfessed, unrepented sin of bitterness is like drinking poison, hoping someone else will die. Often times when we are attacked we react to that attack rather than respond to God. Beloved, God is in control.

> *The unconfessed, unrepented sin of bitterness is like drinking poison, hoping someone else will die.*

I have a personal "apple a day" theory when it comes to these kinds of difficult situations in my relationships.

A -*Apply forgiveness immediately.*

P - *Pray for the person who offended you.*

P - *Praise God you were not the offender.*

L - *Look for the good and what God is saying.*

E - *Encourage somebody whom you know is hurting.*

And if all this is not enough to encourage your heart to do right, here's a great truth that always works for me.

"Great peace have they that love Thy law and nothing shall offend them." [17] Whenever your heart is at peace because you know your vertical and horizontal relationships are right—nothing, and I mean nothing, offends you. Why? Because you know God's thoughts towards you are thoughts of peace and not evil that He might fulfill His purpose in you—and ALL THINGS do work together for good to those who love God. Beloved, He really is large and in charge.

Finally here are two compelling examples of how to handle personal attacks that come from the lives of two famous men: Sir Walter Raleigh and Abraham Lincoln.

As he walked through a public square one day, Sir Walter Raleigh was spit on by a young boy. Wiping the spittle from his face with his handkerchief, he said, "Young man, if I could wipe your blood off my conscious as easy as I could your spittle off my body, I would take your life. But because I can't, I treat you with mercy." The boy was smitten by Sir Walter's response and fell on his knees begging forgiveness.

> *"Great peace have they that love Thy law and nothing shall offend them."*

Abraham Lincoln made a lot of friends and enemies as well. One of his most outspoken enemies was a man named Stanton. He so despised Lincoln that he wrote in a major newspaper that Lincoln was a "low, cunning clown," and said that it was "ridiculous for people to go to Africa to find a gorilla, when they could easily find one in Springfield, Illinois." Despite his scurrilous attacks, Lincoln never tried to defend himself against Stanton. Yet when Lincoln became president, to the astonishment of all, he selected Stanton as his Secretary of War. When asked why, he replied, "Because he is the best man for the job."

When the assassin's bullet had snuffed out Lincoln's life and his body lay in state, Stanton stood before the casket and with tears streaming down his face said, *"There lays the greatest ruler of men this world has ever seen!"* Stanton could not resist the non-retaliating, longsuffering spirit of Lincoln.

Remember, don't let the personal attacks of pests "bug" you to death! Learn to respond to God and not react to the challenge.

Principle Six
Healing Deep Wounds

The deep wounds received from "burned relationships" are to be healed up with new growth and not peeled bare with daily grieving and bitter griping!

Intense forest fires will leave a charred wound on the sequoia, but the tree begins immediately to repair the damage and all the while it continues to grow larger! In the growing season following the fire, the tree will grow slabs of wood thicker than the bark on the rest of the tree in order to cover the burned portion. This unique ability of the redwood/sequoia tree to withstand fire and disease and insect attack accounts for their long life span.

Getting burned in relationships and bruised in our hearts is an inescapable reality of life. However, if wrongly treated, these wounds will lead us into bondage to bitterness. When we get burned in a relationship we do our best to keep from falling apart, losing our minds or reacting in a way that would increase the pain by public embarrassment. We commonly do this by wrapping the wound or bruise in a psychological bandage of suppression that does one of three things:

One, we either assume all the blame and shame and say to ourselves, "You're a bad person and deserve this."

Two, we internalize the hurt and trauma to such an extent that it causes an emotional overload and little or no feelings are experienced. This person lives like an emotional zombie.

Three, we assert control and develop either an "I'm standing on the inside and nothing you can do on the outside will make me sit down" attitude or a dissociation that forms another personality, that is able to take whatever comes and enables the person to block out the hurt by saying this never really happened to me.

All of the above are unbiblical responses to hurts. Wrapping a wound in any of the above bandages provides only temporary relief. Why? Because when we hide the hurt by these wrappings, we shut out the healing light of God's Spirit and God's Word and shut the burn into a position of darkness where it festers and becomes infected and infested. Hurts wrongly treated aren't forgotten and they don't fade away or get fixed with time, but instead they ferment until their "bitter germs" begin to leak through the bandages and affect everything within us and every relationship around us. *"Look after each other so that none of you will miss out on the special favor of God. Watch out that no bitter root of unbelief rises up among you, for whenever it springs up, many are corrupted by its poison."* [1]

> *Getting burned in relationships and bruised in our hearts is an inescapable reality of life.*

*How Mistreated "Heart-burns" Lead into Bondage.
Using the acrostic "HURTS" we discover:*

H – *Horrible experiences* -- These traumatic experiences
may be at hands of loved ones, self-inflicted or just part and
parcel of living in a fallen world.

U – *Unbiblical perception* of hurts creates a wrong pattern
of thinking.

R –*Raise up a stronghold* (anything that has a strong hold
on your mind) to shield and defend your perceptions and
confirm that you're always the exception.

My past makes me an exception (dysfunctional family,
unplanned for, disastrous mistakes, disappointment
and despair).

My pain makes me an exception (abused, abandoned,
illness, loss and accidents).

My poverty makes me an exception (no talents, no training, not very smart, financially impoverished,
deprived).

My poor self-image makes me an exception (never
affirmed, rejected, betrayed, abandoned, unloved, and
unappreciated, told I was ugly, dumb and would never
amount to anything).

T – *Troubles are kept wrapped in darkness* and God's light
and love are kept locked out.

S – *Soul burns* (these are emotional hurts received from
feeling you really got torched in a relationship) are

aggravated and perpetuated to the next generation.

Mistreated "heart burns" or soul-bruises affect all relationships

- They affect the way we relate to God – Unresolved hurts produce persons tormented by guilt and feelings of unworthiness from childhood because they never were able to measure up in the eyes of those who really mattered in their lives. There is a jamming of the signals from heaven that causes them to misinterpret our Heavenly Father and picture Him through the distorted lens of their earthly parents. Yet the truth is, our Father in Heaven is not a reflection of our earthly fathers but the perfection of them! Unresolved hurts motivate the person to operate by grit and determination instead of by grace and Holy Spirit liberation. If you ask this individual what he thinks God thinks about him, his answer is most often in the negative. He feels disappointed in me, He feels I'm not worth anything to His Kingdom.
- They affect the way we relate to ourselves – The heart becomes filled with angry, bitter feelings, feelings of rejection, resentment, a sense of dividedness, of double-mindedness, inability to give or receive love, chronically depressed and often times neurotically perfectionistic.
- They affect relationships with others – They lock you into emotional immaturity. Typical expressions of these hurts are, "I've never gotten over it to this day"; "you just don't understand how deeply I was hurt." This prolonged wrong response to the hurt locks you into acting in this area of your emotions like a little child. The person tends to be fearful of others finding out who they really are and as a

result rejecting them and causing more hurt. They also have a tendency to find someone to listen to their hurts and meet their needs and the person most sympathetic to their needs is the one with similar hurts. The result-two dysfunctional, twisted, hurting, rejected persons marry and neither can give what they don't have. This leads to more dysfunction being passed on to the next generation!

Irrespective of how old, deep, painful, and mishandled your "Heart-burns" or "Soul-Bruises" may be – you can be Healed-up and Freed-up!

I am using another acrostic – *FORGIVES* – to set forth the way to treat the painful burns of torched relationships.

F – Face up to your responsibility

You can't be healed and freed of what you fail to face and surrender.

Stop accusing others and apologizing for yourself (self-handicapping). Shame and blame is the modus operandi of the spirit of rejection that has bruised your soul. You can't be healed and freed of what you fail to face and surrender.

Just remember, admitting your emotional heart burns, bruises and bondages may help define your identity, but if you stop there it will confine you to irresponsibility as always a victim or a mere survivor (I'm an alcoholic, I'm gay, I'm an incest survivor, I'm a bankrupt business person, etc.).

In God's kingdom there is no acceptable excuse for sin.

The fact that others hurt you so deeply and treated you so wrongfully doesn't justify the way you have responded and continue to react. In God's Kingdom there is no acceptable excuse for sin. It's not the devil, your parents, your environment or your genetic predisposition that makes you respond wrongly. It's the choices you continue to make on a daily basis, buying into a lie about who you are!

O – Open the unhealed wound and expose it to the light -- *"And do not participate in the unfruitful deeds of darkness, but instead even expose them;"* [2]

God wants to shine through you to His glory, but opening up our wounded heart is a very humbling process. You are to reduce to rubble the almost impenetrable fortress in which you have encased your heart. As you are faithful to do it from the outside in, God is faithful to do it from the inside out. The healing of your wounded heart is easy for Jesus. Unfortunately, it is very hard for you. Healing requires a return to your roots and these roots you have spent a lifetime covering up with dirt. What you uncover, God covers; but what you cover, God uncovers.

> *What you uncover, God covers; but what you cover, God uncovers.*

Pray this: *Lord, I've wrapped my heart in bandages of my own making. I've tried to treat my own wounds by hiding them from the light. Here and now, once and for all, I open them to you blessed Father.*

R – Release total forgiveness toward those who've hurt you -- *"And his lord, moved with anger, handed him over to the* *torturers until he should repay all that was owed him.* [3] *So shall My heavenly Father also do to you, if each of you does not forgive his brother from your heart."* [4] You mean I must let them off the hook? Yes, unless you do so you are exactly as you just said, "HOOKED" to them via your unforgiveness. Freely you have received forgiveness, freely you for-

> *Freely you have received forgiveness, freely you forgive.*

give. Feelings will come, but forgiveness like love is a choice you alone can make.

G – Guard what you receive – God designed us as receivers. We are a composite of what we have received. We must reject the wrong things and receive the right things. We must reject words that are negative and that try to convince us and control us. We must reject the words of those who would have us believe that we are stupid, unwanted, unloved, unneeded, unworthy, and unwelcome. Whose report will you believe? We'll believe the report of the Lord—what God says about me.

I – Invite the Holy Spirit's Anointing to Break Every Yoke of Bondage and Release His Love to You and Through You -- *"And it shall come to pass in that day, that his burden shall be taken away from off thy shoulder, and his yoke from off thy neck, and the yoke shall be destroyed because of the anointing."* [5] The anointing, (the manifest presence and power of the Holy Spirit) is the power of God that removes the burdens and breaks every yoke of bondage. Jesus said, *"The Spirit of the Lord is upon me, because He has anointed me to heal the broken hearted and set the captives free."*

The Holy Spirit's assignment is to force the issue of control in each and every area of our lives. No comfort zones, no bitterness zones, no lust areas, etc. are allowed to operate in the life of God's people. His control is a must.

V - View yourself as you truly are in Christ not as what you formerly were in yourself -- *"Therefore if any man be in Christ, he is a new creature: old things are passed away; behold, all things are become new."* [6]

You are not unloved or unwanted, but one of the few, the free, and the forgiven! You are not condemned or cursed but chosen of God, called by name by the Holy Spirit and complete in Christ. You are not inferior or superior, but by God's grace, you have become an object of the Holy Spirit's ministry on your interior! Failure is an event in your life. It is not you. You fail a lot but failing in life doesn't mean you're a failure. By the grace of God -- and not by so-called luck of birth or getting all the right breaks or by old-fashioned hard work – you are what you are. And you are that because God says it's so and it's so even if every demon screams, "lie," and every person says, "nay," and my own heart says, "I don't feel it!" Someone has said, "God said it—I believe it—That settles it." Well, that's true in one sense, but not in another. Let me explain. Everything that God says about us is legally, judicially, and positionally true. However, in order for it to be experientially true in every day life, I must believe. So, on one side of that coin (experientially) God said it—I believe it--That settles it; but on the other side of the coin (legally, judicially, and posi-

> *You are not unloved or unwanted, but one of the few, the free, and the forgiven!*

tionally) God said it—That settles it no matter what we believe. God is not a man that He should lie.

E - Embrace your life as a healed, cracked pot of clay through which others may see the Light. *"But we have this treasure in earthen vessels, that the excellence of the power may be of God and not of us."* [7] Paul reminds all believers that the treasure of the gospel and the life that it brings when accompanied by the power of the Holy Spirit is contained in the earthen vessels of our bodies. The word for earthen vessels is that of clay pots. All believers are at best cracked pots of clay in which the light, life and love of God dwells. God's desire is that we allow these things to pour forth through the cracks in our lives. When this happens people do not pay attention to all the bad cracks, but only to the amazing love and light that confirms that it is not who we are but who we contain that makes us vessels of honor for His use.

John Sandford writes: "Christian healing comes then not by making a broken thing good enough to work, but by delivering us from the power of that broken thing so that it can no longer rule us and by teaching us to trust God to shine in and through that very thing."

S - See through the eyes of love and share your love – Because the love of God is for us, around us, upon us and resident within us, we can live and walk in this "atmosphere" daily. The love of God indwelling us is to be the "tie that binds" and the "garment" the Christian is to put on. It is to be the "universal motive" for all that we do. It is to prevent our Christian liberty from turning into destructive selfishness. It is to characterize our preaching and teaching of the truth.

What is love? An eight year old boy got very close to love's meaning when he said, "When my grandmother got arthritis, she couldn't bend over and paint her toenails anymore. So my grandfather does it for her all the time, even when his hands got arthritis too. That's love." The interesting thing about the Bible is that although it uses the words and illustrations of love, many times, it never defines what love is but instead describes what love does. Thus, we can conclude that love is only love when it acts. The kind of love that God is and that He gives– agape love-- is a gracious, determined and active interest in the true welfare of others. God's love is not discouraged even by hatred, cursing or abuse and isn't limited by calculation of what I deserve or results. It is based solely on the nature of God. Whereas eros and philos love are dependent on the value of their object, agape is love that creates value in its object.

Dudley Hall --"God's love is that essence of life that gives without regard to cost to meet the actual needs of another, asking nothing in return!"

John Piper, "Love is the overflow of joy in God that gladly meets the needs of others."

Love is the compassion that cares, the care that gets involved, the commitment that sticks with a people through thick and thin!

Love is risk-taking when the flesh says look out for number one first.

Love is silence—when your words would hurt.

It is patience—when your neighbor's curt.

It is deafness—when a scandal flows.

It is thoughtfulness—for other's woes.
It is promptness—when stern duty calls.
It is courage—when misfortune falls.
Love ever gives, forgives and outlives,
Ever stands with open hands.
And while it lives, It gives, For this is love's prerogative—
  To give, and give, and give!

When I first came on board World Wide Dream Builders as pastor/advisor, there was an awesome sense of my responsibilities to them as an organization. I realized World Wide was primarily a business organization comprised of many differing cultures, races, religious beliefs and some with no beliefs religiously at all. Billie and I were asked to serve in helping with every aspect of human relationships for those in leadership who wanted help (primarily as marriage counselors). Dick Davis (CEO of WWDB) has been invaluable to us in helping navigate these waters. I remember when Billie and I prayed together and accepted this assignment from God through Ron and Georgia Lee Puryear and the World Wide Management Team. Our constant thought was, "Love never fails." No matter how difficult. "Love never fails." When there would be misunderstanding or rejection, "Love never fails." When counsel is refused or rejected, "Love never fails." No matter what a person's background is or what we might not see eye to eye on, "Love never fails." We realized if we were filled with God's love, we would be non-judgmental, non-critical, non-threatening and in the most effective way be empowered by love to help hurting people.

> *Love is risk-taking when the flesh says look out for number one first.*

One day in the beginning of our relationship I shared my heart with Ron Puryear and the Management Team. I said, "If I miss God, I want to miss God on the top side and not the bottom side." By that I mean, I would rather stand before God and have Him say, you know Paul, you just loved too much, forgave too much, were too kind, too longsuffering, too patient, too redemptive. Rather than have Him say, I didn't love enough, forgive enough, etc., etc.

The reason I think this way is because of all the love and forgiveness, kindness, patience and redemption I have received from so many for so long. This has filled my heart with a supernatural love for people that I cannot fully comprehend. All I know is that this kind of love sees with a different mindset. We see men with double vision -- as they are by nature and as they can be by grace. We should be able to see men not as rich or poor, black or white, beautiful or ugly, educated or uneducated; not according to their religion, but only as God sees men and women-- created in His image.

> *"If I miss God, I want to miss God on the top side and not the bottom side."*

A small boy went to the lingerie department of a store to purchase a gift for his mother. Bashfully he told the clerk that he wanted to buy a slip for his mom, but he didn't know her size. The lady explained that it would help if he could describe her. Was she thin, fat, short, tall, or what? "Well," replied the youngster, "she's just about perfect!" So the clerk sent him home with a size 34. A few days later the mother came to the store to exchange the gift. It was too small. She needed a size 52. The little fellow had seen her through the eyes of love, which didn't take into account the exact dimensions of the tape measure. God give us Your eyes to see people the way You see them.

Tom Brown and Rachel Jones were next-door neighbors. They fell in love with each other. At the age of 34 something happened between them that hurt Rachel deeply. She responded wrongly. She refused to talk, period. She hurled herself away from the guy she loved. Every week for 38 years Tom Brown slipped a letter under Rachel's door. Every week Rachel took that letter and promptly tore it up never taking time to read it before dropping it into the waste can. Tom and Rachel got married at the age of 72. What happened? One day Rachel decided, that after 38 persistent years of Tom's letter writing, the least she could do was to read one of the letters. When she opened it, she found a sincere apology, which she received as well as Tom's proposal to become his wife. How foolish you say! Yes, but I wonder how many situations you have been involved in where there has been deep hurt and you have responded wrongly? Instead of opening the situation up and dealing with it, learning how to reorient your mind and manage your mouth and be one who employs the truths of the FORGIVES acrostic, you have responded just like Rachel did. Days have turned into months, months have turned into years, relationships are still soured and you are finding it extremely difficult to have a relationship with anyone to any depth.

Remember, to have SEQUOIA-SIZE SUCCESS, like the giant sequoia, you must consistently deploy the FORGIVES principles toward the painful "burns" of life and those deep wounds received will be healed up with new growth and you will be able to stop peeling them bare with daily grieving and bitter griping!

Principle Seven
Guard Your Roots

Guard your root system from public trampling!

A CNN news report states that in March of 2004, "Two giant sequoias that put down roots long before the United States became a country fell, the first of the age-old forest titans to fall in years. The trees, thought to be between 300 years and 750 years old, were located in a grove along the Yosemite National Park's southern border. The park has hundreds of giant sequoias in three large groves."

"Soil or root failure caused the collapse of at least one of the trees, which may have toppled the second sequoia as it fell," Park Ranger Deb Schweizer said. A young sequoia in the grove fell in 1998. Before that, the last sequoia known to have fallen in the park was in 1969. Schweizer said, *"Foot traffic around the base of the fallen trees could have damaged the root systems and contributed to the collapse."* Park officials have been surrounding some of the oldest, largest and most historically significant trees with fences to *"keep the public from trampling root systems,"* Schweizer said.

Wow! Even giant trees that have lived for hundreds of years cannot survive when there is no sacred enclosure around its root system! If this is true for trees, how much more must it be true of humans? No matter how tightly our roots are woven together, we must protect ourselves from such trampling. In light of the way the sacred has been trampled into the ground today, one often hears people ask, "Is there nothing sacred anymore?"

Those who choose to live without a sacred enclosure around their life and allow the root system of their lives to be trampled by the public are in danger of great devastation. We must guard our life against handling our birthright in a light and irreverent manner. God has given us great and mighty promises; we must not take them lightly. God has extended unconditional love. We must not grieve His heart. God has given unconditional acceptance, we must not take that for granted. God has extended unconditional forgiveness, we must not use that as license. Some people seem to ascribe to that false adage, "It's a lot easier to get forgiveness than permission." The truth is, whenever we don't guard our hearts and minds, we allow seeds of doubt and destruction to be planted. Many a person who began well did not end well. Something happened in the middle. Might I humbly suggest that possibly they began to treat the holy things of God in a light manner. God will not be taken for granted. There is a glaring example in Genesis of a man who did exactly that. His name was Esau.

> *God has given us great and mighty promises; we must not take them lightly.*

Esau demonstrated his unbelief, not by cursing, but by demonstrating that there was nothing sacred and truly valuable to him. We read in Genesis that he *"sold his birthright unto Jacob."* [1] In a moment of hunger, Esau sold to his brother the birthright privileges of the firstborn. Modern Westerners are tempted to ask, "So, what's the big deal?" But in Biblical times the Jewish birthright and the patriarchal privileges of the first born were tremendous and God-sanctioned. The rights and privileges of the first born included a position of honor, of authority, of priestly service, of material blessings (the firstborn received double the inheritance of the rest of the heirs) and a position of prophetic blessing. All of these privileges should have been highly prized by Esau. These were blessings of great and eternal value!

Yet, having no guard about the root system of what is truly valuable, he treated as common these God-given blessings and sold them for a bowl of red soup! What a demonstration of unbelief! What carelessness!

What did Esau do that was so wrong? He treated the God-imparted root system of values and that which has eternal worth as something cheap and common. This doesn't mean that Esau cursed and used God's name in vain. Instead it means that he treated everything as common and that spiritual things found no place in his life. He lived

> *Many of us treat as worthless that which is of great value.*

for the moment, for instant gratification, for sensual enjoyments. Sacred things became common. He chose physical gratification over spiritual blessings. There were values to be prized but he treated them lightly. He was a man who didn't care.

A story is told of a man who loved old books. He met an

acquaintance that had just thrown away a Bible that had been stored in the attic of his ancestral home for generations. "I couldn't read it," the friend explained. "Somebody named Guten-something or other had printed it."

"Not Gutenberg!" the book lover exclaimed in horror. "That Bible was one of the first books ever printed. Why, a copy just recently sold for over two million dollars!"

His friend was unimpressed. "Mine wouldn't have brought a dollar. Some fellow named Martin Luther had scribbled all over it in German."

Martin Luther just happened to be one of the great leaders of the historical Reformation. He was also the founder of the Lutheran denomination. This alone would make this particular Bible of untold value. Like this man, many of us treat as worthless that which is of great value.

Years ago, I heard a man talk about life being a trade-off. He went on to say, if you are going to trade off, always trade up, not down. Trade your time for something of worth and value. In other words, use what God has given you in every area to invest in what God invests. PEOPLE.

STOP! LOOK! LISTEN! You and I can never be successful if we have no sacred enclosure around what is truly valuable in life. If we allow the world system with all its allurements to trample into every area of our lives, we, like the giant sequoias that CNN reported as having fallen in 2004, will also fall and take many with us in the process.

No Regrets. That's the heart cry of every person that dreams of a life of abundance and success. This does not happen by accident, but only when we live intentionally—on purpose. Don't live another day with regret. Learn from them but move on without its baggage.

> *No Regrets. That's the heart cry of every person that dreams of a life of abundance and success.*

Dwight Bain writes about The City of Regret.

I had not really planned to take a trip this year, yet I found myself packing anyway. And off I went, dreading it. I was on another guilt trip.

*I booked my reservation on **Wish I Had Airlines**. I didn't check my bags—everyone carried their baggage on this airline—and had to drag it for what seemed like miles in the Regret City Airport. And I could see that people from all over the world were there with me, limping along under the weight of bags they had packed themselves.*

*I caught a cab to **Last Resort Hotel**, the driver taking the whole trip backward, looking over his shoulder. And there I found the ballroom where my event would be held: **the Annual Pity Party**. As I checked in, I saw that all my old colleagues were on the guest list:*

The Done family—Woulda, Coulda, and Shoulda and both of the Opportunities—Missed and Lost.

All the Yesterdays—there were too many to count, but all would have sad stories to share.

Shattered Dreams and Broken Promises would be there, too, along with their friends, Don't Blame Me and Couldn't Help It.

*And of course, hours and hours of entertainment would be provided by that renowned storyteller **It's Their Fault**.*

*As I prepared to settle in for a really long night, I realized that one person had the power to send all those people home and break up the party: **Me**. All I had to do was take ownership and personal responsibility for my own life.*

If you found yourself getting on a flight to the City of Regret, recognize that it's a trip you book yourself, and you can cancel it at any time—without penalty or fee. But you're the only one who can.

There are danger zones in the life of any leader. These are times when we need to guard our hearts in a special way. *"Be sober, be vigilant because your adversary, the devil, as a roaring lion, walks about, seeking whom he may devour: whom resist steadfast in faith knowing others like you have the same kind of opposition."* [2] Words I like here are be sober, which means be serious about guarding your life. Be vigilant which means be sincere about guiding your life. Finally, whom resist. Dear reader, we are not laboring toward victory, but from victory to victory. When we submit ourselves to God seriously and sincerely, then we can resist every enemy, and he will flee from us.

Listed below are several times when the enemy seems to intensify his assault.

- After a victory you have been believing God for.
- When you are alone.
- When you are physically drained.
- When you are waiting on an answer to prayer.
- When you are going to a major function.

- When you are serious about a brand new commitment to your dream.
- When you take God's promises seriously.

Some of the ways that I would suggest for you to avoid public trampling on your roots are through proper stewardship:

- S - Submission to authorities in your life.
- T - Teachable spirit towards those mentoring you.
- E - Edifiable because of the way you conduct your life.
- W - Willingness to be corrected.
- A - Accountable to God, yourself and those you have asked to be honest with you.
- R - Repentant immediately.
- D - Determination to finish well.

We live in the greatest land of promise. Don't end up being a prisoner in the Promised Land.

There is a tragic story that illustrates having the means to escape but not acting upon it. In his historical book *The Three Edwards*, Thomas Costaine described such a tragedy.

During the fourteenth century a duke named Ranald lived in the region which is now Belgium. Ranald was grossly overweight. In fact, he was commonly called by his Latin nickname 'Crassis,' which means fat. Eventually Ranald became the king, but his brother Edward, was very jealous. After a violent quarrel, Edward rallied a group of people together and led a revolt, taking over the castle and the kingdom.

Now you would think the younger Edward would kill his

older brother, as was often done, but somehow he had compassion on the hefty guy and built a dungeon for him—a very specific kind of dungeon. Edward removed Ranald from the throne and built a large circular room, which had a doorway but no door. Inside the room was a bed and table and all the essentials Ranald would need. The doorway to the room was a regular-sized doorway but Ranald was too big to get through it. Edward placed Ranald in the room and said, 'When you can fit through the doorway, you can leave.'

Every day Edward would have his servants bring to the room a smorgasbord of pies and pastries, along with massive platters of meat and other delicacies and lay it all out in front of old 'Crassis.' People used to accuse Edward of being a cruel king, but Edward had a ready answer. **"My brother is not a prisoner. He can leave when he chooses to."**

Ranald remained in that same room, a prisoner of his own appetite, for more than ten years. He wasn't released until after Edward died in battle. By then his own health was so far gone that he died within a year. He died not because he had no choice, but because he would not use his power to choose what was best for his life.

A person must realize that most failures are self-imposed. Most prisons are of our own design. Most people that do not end well have been led astray by their own unrestrained passions. So we must:

- Be alert.
- Be discerning.
- Be God-controlled.

- Be armed.
- Be prudent.
- Be prayerful.

Guard Your Root System from Public Trampling!

Principle Eight
Think Generationally

There is no success without a successor, so think generationally!

The redwood/sequoia burls (a large rounded outgrowth on the trunk or branch of a tree) are another survival strategy. Their growth is held in check by the presence of chemical signals in a living sequoia. If the tree should die, or even be stressed by low rainfall or fire, the chemical signal weakens or vanishes and the burl will burst forth into verdant life.

> *"There is no success without a successor."*

Burls kept in a shallow pan of water will grow almost indefinitely. They can also continue on to become a full-grown redwood/sequoia tree. These giant trees are genetically programmed to reproduce successors.

Peter Drucker was right when he stated: **"There is no success without a successor."** After you have done everything you can to help your leaders and they are getting the job done, you may think you're finished. NOT! There is still one more step you must take to complete the process. You have to help them learn to repeat the development process and teach others to repeat the process because lasting success comes only when every generation continues to develop the next generation. Duplicate your efforts by training others to be successful in your business. Build for others and turn your purpose in life into a legacy.

"The final test of a leader," says Walter Lippmann, "is that he leaves behind him in others the conviction and the will to carry on."

Build for others and turn your purpose in life into a legacy.

Even the word passion when broken down reminds us of our responsibility. Pass I On. Mentorship is one of the most important aspects of a great leader. Only those who have stepped into those shoes know how difficult and at times how inconvenient this role can be. Without mentorship, we pass on a large gaping hole to our successor. For those who are being mentored, allow me to make a few suggestions. First and foremost, treasure your mentor. Next, don't try to impress him. He's been there.

- Your Mentor is a major gift from God to you.
- Your Mentor is someone God has placed close to you to unlock your greatness.

Mentors are more than teachers.

- Teachers love information.
   Mentors love protegés.
- Teachers love education.
   Mentors love impartation.
- Teachers study to learn.
   Mentors study to sow.
- **Mentors are not necessarily cheerleaders; they are**

coaches. Their role is not merely to confirm what you are doing correctly. Their goal is to correct you and prevent you from making a mistake.

- **You may have more than one Mentor in your life, but there is usually a primary mentor.** This primary mentor will usually remain with you throughout your life. Different levels of mentorship exist. We are mentored through tapes, books and relationships.

- **Don't take access to your Mentor lightly.** He may not always be there. You must face some battles alone. So drink deeply from his well now while you have access.

- **Treasure any invitation to be alone with your Mentor.** The presence of others changes the flow of information. When I am alone with my mentor, I receive much more information than I do when others are present. The information is more specific. Exact. Precise. Just for me. The thoughts and opinions of others present often dilute and even weaken the impartation.

- **Your Mentor often knows instantly whether you discern his worth or not.** No words need to be spoken. Flattering words are unnecessary. Persuasive words do not matter.

> *Mentors are not necessarily cheerleaders; they are coaches.*

- **A Mentor knows how much you value and respect his counsel by how you respond to it.** *"A wise son heeds his father's instructions."*[1]

I believe there is only one way to bridge the gap to the next generation of leaders. So let's talk about generational transfer.

Generational Transfer Requires Developing a Father's Heart and Passing it on to Sons.

True fathers impart a sense of identity to their sons; a sense of duty; of destiny and do everything in their power to equip their sons to mature to become reproducing fathers themselves.

Dennis Peacocke points out that "lasting wealth is multi-generational and is oriented toward the long-run and not the short-run. This is why generational wealth often disappears in two or three generations. It isn't stolen; it's mismanaged ... and so it is with a legacy."

The Process of Generational Transfer Requires Imitating the Pattern Son Jesus.

When it comes to the concept of generational transfer, Jesus is the ultimate leader and model. During His life on earth, he took twelve men (one of which turned out to be a failure) and transformed three years of

> *Generational transfer requires developing a father's heart and passing it on to sons.*

personal investment in their lives into a worldwide movement that forever changed and continues to change history. Today, more people follow Him than any other leader in the world. As a model leader, Jesus practiced the most vital principles of leadership—and He provided an example for us to imitate.

Someone used the acrostic – **IDEA** – to show how Jesus mentored men:

I - Instruction in a life related context. He taught them with his words.

D - Demonstration in a life related context. He taught them by His example.

E - Experience in a life related context. He taught them with their own experience.

A - Assessment in a life related context. He taught them through evaluating their growth.

Borrowing from Robert Coleman, I am setting forth some concepts that Jesus employed that are strategic for generational transfer. This model will work in the spiritual arena of making disciples, in the family for extending the legacy and in a business for insuring succession.

Irrespective of what you personally believe about Jesus, the impact of his leadership is undeniable. Using Jesus as the model, we discover that the first concept for reproducing successors is:

(1)   Selection for Vocation— "...he choose twelve men..." [2]

He selected twelve men and began to train them for their future vocation of doing with others what He would be doing with them. Men were his method. Generational transfer isn't by programs, but by people; not by institutions, but by individuals; not by books, but by believers.

Jesus' ministry reached thousands and touched thousands, but He trained twelve men. He gave His life on the cross for millions, but He gave His three years of public life to twelve men. Miracles, multitudes and mass ministry benefited from Jesus' work, but they didn't constitute His work. Men were His work. Jesus saw the masses through the man, and He built the man to impact the masses.

Leaders must *choose* to develop their key people. Effective leaders know those who are closest to them impact their success. They do not leave this issue to chance or to the votes of executive committees. Instead, they carefully select who will be on their team and give great attention to the details of who will play crucial roles and what roles they will play on that team. Jesus never left His choices up to popularity polls or majority vote. He made deliberate choices about everything and even stayed up all night praying before He chose His disciples.

> *Leaders must choose to develop their key people.*

What did He look for in selecting a person? He looked for a **F-A-T-S-O** type individual. These are those that He saw as having the potential to develop into *Faithful – Available – Teachable - Servant-spirited – Obedient persons.*

The second phase of Jesus' method for generational transfer was:

(2) Association for Infection -- "... He chose twelve that they might be with Him...". [3] Whatever the leader has is what his followers are going to get. The process of developing leaders to succeed us is a process that is better caught than taught. Yes, we must always be at least a step ahead in order to lead others, but we must not make ourselves unapproachable. There is a frequent association that is essential if we want to pass on our DNA to those that we want to carry on when we are gone. There must be personal, intimate, long-term association for the purpose of infection and impartation of life as well as learning.

Impact comes from relationships not positions. "A new commandment I give to you, that you love one another, even as I have loved you, that you also love one another. By this will all men know that you are my disciples, if you have love for one another." [4] Jesus knew the importance of relationships, and He never depreciated the importance of one person over masses of people. He did not build a royal palace and set up a throne in it and declare, "This is my palace and it's the only place you can see Me, and then only at big

Impact comes from relationships not positions.

church meetings at a distance." Jesus went in to the marketplace, the boats of fishermen, the Temple, the synagogues and to the homes of all types of persons. He went all over Palestine and as He *"went through the towns, He went about doing good, making disciples."* [5]

If you were asked to name one of the most renowned and influential names in the game of golf, you would probably never mention the name of Harvey Penick. His name never appeared on a winner's trophy at a PGA golf tournament, but when Penick died at the age of 90, the world of golf lost one of its greatest teachers. Although his books have sold millions of copies (and the publication of them almost never occurred, because of his modesty), he was remembered most for his direct impact on people. An *Associated Press* story stated, "Penick refused to teach methods or group lessons, instead applying his wisdom to the talents of individual players." Tom Kite, the leading money winner in PGA Tour history, was 13 when he began working with Penick. Ben Crenshaw began learning the game from Penick at the age of 6. Any golf fan of today will have etched on his memory the picture of Crenshaw on his knees on the eighteenth green of Augusta National Golf Course after sinking the winning putt in the 1995 Masters Golf Tournament. Crenshaw was in tears and he stated that his week at the Masters was emotionally wrenching to him, not merely because of the pressure of tournament competition, but also because his lifelong teacher, Harvey Penick, had died that week. Penick, who could have spent his life speaking to crowds, chose instead to invest himself in individual persons — many of them children — one at a time.

The Apostle Paul modeled this kind of unselfish discipling or mentoring with a mission, with a young man named Timothy. Then he urged Timothy to do the same with others. He wrote, *"The things that you have heard from me...commit these to faithful men who will be able to teach others also."* [6]

Another step in the process of achieving success via successors that Jesus employed was:

(3) Demonstration for Instruction— *"For I have given you an example, that you should do as I have done to you."* [7] Teaching, training, and transforming are the basis for all generational transfer. Someone described the process as: "Tell them what; tell them why; show them how; do it with them; let them do it; and then deploy them." Laura Chamberlain demonstrates Jesus approach in this way:

1. *He modeled - He did it.* [8]
2. *He mentored - He did it and they were with Him.* [9]
3. *He monitored - They did it and He was with them.* [10]
4. *He motivated - They did it and He was in the background encouraging them.* [11]
5. *He multiplied - They did it.* [12]

(4) Delegation for Dream Penetration — *"After these things the Lord appointed seventy others also, and sent them two by two before His face into every city and place where He Himself was about to go."* [13] After Jesus had cast His visions and goals for His mission, He didn't try to be a one man show, but delegated responsibility and sent them out on assigned jobs.

> *Teaching, training, and transforming are the basis for all generational transfer.*

There will be no generational transfer in the family, the family business or in the church if we don't empower those we are raising up to do what we are doing with the freedom to expand the vision and do it better and more extensively.

C. S. Lewis described one of the basic frustrations of generational transfer when he wrote: "In a sort of ghastly simplicity we remove the organ and demand the function. We make men without chests and expect of them virtue and enterprise. We laugh at honor and are shocked to find traitors in our midst. We castrate and bid the gelding be fruitful." We must raise up real "stallions" for the future that will be able to reproduce the righteous standard that we have established in our family, businesses and churches for generations to come.

(5) *Supervision for Correction and Continuation* — *"But Jesus, being aware of it, said to them, "Why do you reason because you have no bread? Do you not yet perceive nor understand? Is your heart still hardened?"* [13] These words are a rebuke to his disciples for failing to grasp what He had been trying to teach them.

From Jesus' ministry and leadership style we can see that He kept check on them. *He used the basic principles of repetition, application and correction.* We must employ these same principles in love and teach those we are raising up to be our possible successors that correction isn't rejection.

(6) *Reproduction for Generational Transfer* – *"You did not choose Me, but I chose you and appointed you that you should go and bear fruit, and that your fruit should remain, that whatever you ask the Father in My name He may give you."* [14]

Jesus expected His men in training for reigning with Him to grow out of a childhood consumerism. His desire for them was to become producers and then reproducers that imparted the vision, a sense of identity and destiny to their sons. He expected them to be captured by the vision that He had cast – a vision that was God-planned, God-big and eternity long.

Was He successful? Yes, in fact so successful that within less than one hundred years of His death and resurrection into heaven, the entire known world had been reached with the gospel.

Tertullian, an educated man who would become the great apologist of his time, converted to Christianity in his mid-life years. Many scholars believe the courage of Christian martyrs moved him to accept their faith. His earliest known work is a letter of solace and encouragement to imprisoned Christians awaiting execution. Shortly after that, he sent a long letter to the Roman authorities mocking their attempts to suppress Christianity. "We are but of yesterday," he wrote, "but we have filled every place among you—cities, islands, fortresses, towns, market places, the very camp, tribes, companies, palace, senate, forum—we have left nothing to you but the temples of your gods." Roman persecutors thought if they killed Christians, they could wipe out the church. Tertullian replied with a line for which he has become famous: "The blood of the martyrs is seed." "The more Rome killed," argued Tertullian, "the more people would be converted by the courageous witness of Christians."

Wow! Whatever happened to that type of attitude toward our life assignment as visionaries? Could it be that we have lost the vision of victory? Could it be that we have lost our sense of destiny? We have been created for greatness with the heart of a warrior. Knowing that when we embrace our assignment with conviction, passion and resolve, future generations will be impacted with something worth passing on.

The following illustration will serve as a fitting

conclusion to the challenge to change the world by an ever-expanding generational transfer of men and women who get on their heart what God has on His – the WHOLE WIDE WORLD!

When Apple Computer fell on difficult days a while back, Apple's young chairman, Steven Jobs, traveled from the Silicon Valley to New York City. His purpose was to convince Pepsico's John Sculley to move west and run his struggling company. As the two men overlooked the Manhattan skyline from Sculley's penthouse office, the Pepsi executive started to decline Jobs' offer. "Financially," Sculley said, "you'd have to give me a million-dollar salary, a million-dollar bonus and a million-dollar severance." Flabbergasted. Jobs gulped and agreed—if Sculley would move to California. But Sculley would commit only to being a consultant from New York. At that, Jobs issued a challenge to Sculley—"Do you want to spend the rest of your life selling sugared water or do you want to change the world?"

In his autobiography Odyssey, Sculley admits Jobs' challenge "knocked the wind out of me." He said he had become so caught up with his future at Pepsi, his pension and whether his family could adapt to life in California that an opportunity to "change the world" nearly passed him by. Instead, he put his life in perspective and went to Apple.

We are challenged to change the world one person at a time. It's time we quit messing around with sugared water and begin to allow God to use us all for the sake of our generation and generations to come!

Principle Nine
Aim High

The key to successful personal growth is to daily hunger and thirst for more!

The Coastal Redwoods/Sequoias thrive on and in fact require the heavy fogs that are normal daily occurrences along the coast. These 300-foot plus giants actually pull moisture into their needles at the tops of the tree where the circulation system of the tree can't pump up. The 50-60 degree average temperature of the area is also important to the life cycle of these trees. Due to these two conditions, restrictions are placed on the modern day range of these awesome giants. Although they will grow almost anywhere in America, they will never attain their true size and stature without the Coastal fogs and temperatures that nurture them and at the same time keep other competing species, such as pines, stunted and sodden.

At the sapling stage (75-100 years old) the Giant Sequoia grows very fast and they grow with a narrow pointed top (spire crown). The spire crown makes sure that the sun will reach at least part of each crown so the tree can grow. The trees will keep the spire crowns for a hundred years or more until they are as much as 150 feet off the ground and then the tops begin to flatten out due to the dense and heavy limbs near the top. This is what makes the Giant Sequoia easy to distinguish from other redwoods, pine or fir trees.

The implications of these facts concerning the sequoias are absolutely strategic to successful growth and fruitful, long lasting life. We must live above the mundane and the mediocre and aim to die climbing ever onward and upward.

There is an old hymn that beautifully expresses this type of goal for living in the heavenlies with God:

I'm pressing on the upward way, new heights I'm gain-
ing everyday;
Still praying as I onward bound, Lord plant my feet on
higher ground.
Lord lift me up and let me stand by faith on heaven's sta-
ble land;
A higher plain than I have found, Lord plant my feet on
higher ground.

We must look for our daily bread, for the water of life, for the reason for our being. We must catch the morning dew of the freshness and fullness of Life and be determined to live our lives open before a loving God, whose face is toward us and has a smile of acceptance upon it!

> *We must look for our daily bread, for the water of life, for the reason for our being.*

Author and philosopher, O.S. Guinness has said of the Puritans in American history that they lived as if they stood before an *"Audience of ONE."* This means that they lived their lives in the consciousness of an All-Seeing, All-Powerful, Ever-Present God whose Unshakable Kingdom had become a present reality in their daily living. Their conduct was determined by the awareness that they had been interactively joined with the dynamic, unseen, divine reality of the king- dom of God among them and within them. Because of this awareness, they knew that they were always

> *Being consistently conscious of standing before an audience of One enables us to live a towering lifestyle in the pursuit of excellence.*

totally at home and safe regardless of what was happening in the visible dimensions of the world around them.

Isaiah records five titles given to this audience of One that make life liveable:

His name shall be called Wonderful, Counselor, The mighty God, The everlasting Father, The Prince of Peace. [1]

- **Wonderful**—This takes care of the Dullness of Life—My Need—Of being significant, so that my life has meaning. Our boredom can give way to His wonders!
- **Counselor**—This takes care of the Decisions of Life—My Need—Of bearings straight so that I know where I'm going. Our confusion can give way to His counsel!
- **Mighty God**—This takes care of the Demands of Life—My Need—Of becoming strengthened to meet all of life's demands. Our sense of inadequacy can give way to His power!

- **Everlasting Father**—This takes care of the Dimensions of Life—My Need—Of belonging securely to a forever family. Our temporary relationships and time pressures can give way to His Forever Fatherhood in a Forever Family! Our sense of being orphaned can give way to His Fatherly care.

- **Prince of Peace**—This takes care of the Disturbances of Life—My Need—Of behaving serenely from a heart that's no longer at war with God, itself or others and believing surely that the future is fixed and it's fabulous! Our sense of conflict can give way to His peace!

> *What an excellent life God has arranged for us all. This is the very reason we should strive for personal excellence in all we do.*

The American Heritage Dictionary defines *excellence* as, "The state, quality, or condition of excelling; superiority." The word excel is defined as, "to do or be better than; surpass; to show superiority, surpass others." The words excel, surpass, exceed, transcend, outdo, outstrip all suggest the concept of going beyond a limit or standard.

Because competition or being better than others is a prominent part of the above definitions, it would be easy to misinterpret this and use the world system's standard of climbing and clawing one's way to the top and thus proving they are superior to all others. However, this pursuing of excellence is not a quest for personal superiority, but an opportunity to demonstrate the excellency of faithfulness in all that we put our hands to. Someone remarked that "the pursuit of excellence is gratifying and healthy. The pursuit of perfection is frustrating, neurotic, and a terrible waste of time."

Brian Harbour picks up on this issue in *Rising Above the Crowd*: "Success means being the best. Excellence means being your best. Success to many, means being better than everyone else. Excellence means being better tomorrow than you were yesterday. Success means exceeding the achievements of other people. Excellence means matching your practice with your potential."

> *Someone remarked that "the pursuit of excellence is gratifying and healthy. The pursuit of perfection is frustrating, neurotic, and a terrible waste of time."*

As you read the following verses, it should be clear that God wants His people to abound or excel both in what they are (inward character) and in what they do (behavior or good deeds). It would seem obvious that there is simply no way one can love God with all his heart without seeking to do his or her best.

"Whatever your hand finds to do, do it with all your might, for in the grave, where you are going, there is neither working nor planning nor knowledge nor wisdom." [2]

"So whether you eat or drink or whatever you do, do it all for the glory of God." [3]

"But just as you excel in everything--in faith, in speech, in knowledge, in complete earnestness and in your love for us - see that you also excel in this grace of giving." [4]

"And this is my prayer: that your love may abound more and more in knowledge and depth of insight, so that you may be able to discern what is best and may be pure and blameless until the day of Christ," [5]

"May the Lord make your love increase and overflow for each other and for everyone else, just as ours does for you." [6]

"Finally, brothers, we instructed you how to live in order to please God, as in fact you are living. Now we ask you and urge you in the Lord Jesus to do this more and more." [7]

"And in fact, you do love all the brothers throughout Macedonia. Yet we urge you, brothers, to do so more and more." [8]

We have devoted a section at the end of this book to a list of additional verses that prove to any reasonable person that God's intention is to prosper and bless us, according to His definition of success.

God made us to magnify and put His excellence and glory on display the way a telescope magnifies the stars. We were designed to put the excellence of His goodness, truth, beauty, justice, wisdom and love on display in every area of our lives.

Living with excellence is demonstrated not by how large a house we live in or how big our bank accounts are, but by how much we demonstrate in our daily lives and labors, the worth of our God.

Far too many people live with very little expectation, or else with wrong expectations. Instead of expecting to see and enjoy God and the favor of God, they believe he frowns on them all the time. Instead of expecting that the best is always ahead, they live in dread that the worst is always just around the cor-

Far too many people live with very little expectation.

ner and even when things are going well, they can't enjoy it because they are expecting that it's just too good to last.

The title of Steve Sampson's book is so true: *"Those Who Expect Nothing Are Never Disappointed!"*

What are you expecting? Not much? – then you won't be disappointed, but you will be disillusioned, dejected, depressed, defeated and soured on life.

- When fearful situations develop, why not begin now to expect the opposite—expect faith to rise and replace fear.
- When depression comes rolling in like a heavy rain, why not begin now to expect the opposite— expect joy to rise up from within like a river.
- When sickness attacks your body, why not begin

now to expect the opposite – God's healing power to touch you.

- When lack comes – why not begin now to expect the opposite – expect God's provision and abundance.

- When worry and anxiety get a strangle hold on your heart – why not begin now to expect the opposite – expect God's peace and promises to go on keeping you in calmness with much assurance.

- When relationships are stretched – why not begin now to expect the opposite – expect that even our disagreements will work to deepen our relationship.

How then should we live? We should live expecting everyday in every way the ongoing favor of the Lord. When times are good, confess, "I'm blessed and highly favored of the Lord!" When times are tough and problems abound, confess, "I'm blessed, highly favored of God!" When others get miracles and things get better and you seem to get a bigger mess and more pains, still confess, "I'm blessed, and highly favored of the Lord! And I've been picked out to be picked on to demonstrate that God doesn't have to pet, pamper, prosper, praise and promote me as an indication of my standing with Him. By faith I declare that everything God has promised He will perform! Therefore I will pray from favor, think in terms of favor, translate every event in light of favor and talk of the favor of the Lord!"

> *By faith I declare that everything God has promised He will perform!*

What God says I am, I am. What he says I have, I have.

What He says I can do, I can do by grace through faith!

Therefore I will daily live in humility, availability and responsibility before Him! And with a good confession daily, I will join God's side, because if God be for me, who can be against me.

THIS IS A GREAT CONFESSION TO MAKE DAILY:

UNBELIEF SAYS:

Some other time—but not now.
Some other person—but not me.
Some other dream—but not mine.

I NOW REPENT OF THE SIN OF UNBELIEF:

And believe by faith:
That anything God did at any other time,
He'll do now.
And anything God did through any other person,
He'll do through me.
And any other dream that God made a reality,
He'll make a reality for me.
So, I ask you Lord—to do it--at this time-- for me—
TO MOVE ME INTO MY DESTINY.

REMEMBER:
What the mind can conceive,
The heart can believe,
And God can achieve.

There is a little poem I came across years ago that describes far too many people. It is entitled *"Never Lived."*

> *Never Lived*
> *There was a very cautious man,*
> *who never laughed or played.*
> *He never risked, he never tried,*
> *He never sang or prayed.*
> *And when he one day passed away,*
> *His insurance was denied.*
> *For since he never really lived,*
> *They claimed he never died.*

God has provided everything we need in abundance. Why delay any further? Seize your divine moments, fulfill your destiny and live a life of no regrets.

Prior to a coronation of the Queen of England, a summons is sent to her friends and dignitaries that reads like this:

"We greet you well. Whereas we have appointed the second day of June for the solemnity of our coronation, these are therefore to will and command, all excuses set apart, that you make your personal attendance upon us, at the time above mentioned, there to do and perform such services as shall be required of you." All excuses set apart!

One greater than the Queen of England bids you to "set apart all excuses" and discover the exhilaration of having SEQUOIA-SIZE SUCCESS.

Scripture for
Blessing & Prosperity

Genesis 39:2, "The Lord was with Joseph, and he prospered."

Joshua 1:7, "That thou mayest prosper withersoever thou goest."

Joshua 1:8, "You will be prosperous and successful."

Deuteronomy 8:18, "But remember the Lord your God, for it is He who gives you the ability to produce wealth that He may establish His covenant."

Deuteronomy 28:11, "The Lord will grant you abundant prosperity."

Deuteronomy 28:13, "You will always be at the top, never at the bottom."

Deuteronomy 30:5, "He will make you more prosperous."

Deuteronomy 30:9, "The Lord will again delight in you and make you prosperous."

Psalms 1:1-3, "Blessed is the man who does not walk in the counsel of the wicked or stand in the way of sinners or sit in the seat of mockers. But his delight is in the law of the Lord and on His law he meditates day and night. He is like a tree planted by streams of water, which yields its fruit in season and whose leaf does not wither. Whatever he does prospers."

Psalms 25:13, "He will spend his days in prosperity."

Psalms 35:27, "Let the Lord be magnified, which hath pleasure in the prosperity of His servant."

Proverbs 11:10, "When the righteous prosper the city rejoices."

Proverbs 11:25, "A generous man will prosper."

Proverbs 13:21, "Prosperity is the reward of the righteous."

Proverbs 28:25, "He who trusts in the Lord will prosper."

Jeremiah 29:11, "For I know the plans I have for you,' declares the Lord, 'plans to prosper you'."

John 10:10, "I am come that they might have life, and that they might have it more abundantly."

1 Corinthians 16:2, "On the first day of the week let every one of you lay by him in store, as God has prospered him."

Ephesians 3:20, "Now to Him that is able to do exceeding abundantly above all that we ask or think, according to the power that works in us."

2 Peter 1:3, "According as His divine power has given to us all things that pertain to life and godliness."

3 John 2, "Beloved, I wish above all things that you may prosper and be in health, even as your soul prospers."

Scriptures used
throughout the book.

What is Sequioa-Size Success?
[1]Hebrews 4:1
[2]I Corinthians 2:9
[3]Ecclesiastes 5:18-19
[4]Malachi 3:8
[5]I Corinthians 4:5
[6]Psalm 1:1
[7]Psalm 1:3
[8]Joshua 1:8
[9]Psalm 1:1-3

Principle One: Don't Despise Small Beginnings
[1]Zechariah 4:10

Principle Two: Don't Despise Small Beginnings
[1]Ecclesiastes 4:9
[2]Ecclesiastes 4:12
[3]Psalm 133:1-3
[4]James 5:16a
[5]Ephesians 4:16
[6]Romans 1:12
[7]Galatians 6:2
[8]Galatians 6:1

[9]Colossians 3:12
[10]Luke 6:36
[11]Philippians 2:2-6

Principle Three:
[1]Proverbs 10:9
[2]Proverbs 11:3
[3]I Chronicles 29;17
[4]Titus 2:7-8

Principle Four:
[1]Isaiah 43:2
[2]Jeremiah 17:8
[3]I Peter 4:12
[4]Jeremiah 17:8
[5]Hebrews 12:11
[6]Galatians 6:9

Principle Five:
[1]Matthew 10:16
[2]John 5:31
[3]Matthew 22:18
[4]Matthew 5:38-39
[5]Matthew 5:44-45
[6]2 Corinthians 5:16-19
[7]Matthew 6:14-15
[8]Job 9:3-5
[9]Romans 16:19
[10]Philippians 2:15
[11]James 3:17
[12]Titus 3:2
[13]2 Timothy 2:24

[14]2 Samuel 12
[15]Exodus 21:23-25
[16]Matthew 5:38-39
[17]Psalm 119:165

Principle Six:
[1]Hebrews 12:15
[2]Ephesians 5:11
[3]Matthew 18:34
[4]Matthew 18:35
[5]Isaiah 10:27
[6]2 Corinthians 5:17
[7]2 Corinthians 4:7

Principle Seven:
[1]Genesis 25:33
[2]2 Peter 5:8-9

Principle Eight:
[1]Proverbs 13:1
[2]Mark 3:14a
[3]Mark 3:14b
[4]John 13:34
[5]Acts 10:38
[6]2 Timothy 2:2
[7]John 13:15
[8]Mark 1,2
[9]Mark 3:13-15
[10]Mark 6:7-13
[11]Mark 16;15-18
[12]Acts 1:6-7; 2 Timothy 2:2
[13]Luke 10:1

[14]Mark 8:17
[15]John 15:16

Principle Nine:
[1]Isaiah 9:6
[2]Ecclesiastes 9:10
[3]1 Corinthians 10:31
[4]2 Corinthians 8:7
[5]Philippians 1:9-10
[6]1 Thessalonians 3:12
[7]1 Thessalonians 4:1
[8]1 Thessalonians 4:10
[9]Isaiah 9:6

For additional resources from Paul Tsika Ministries, Inc. write:

Restoration Ranch
P. O. Box 136
Midfield, TX 77458

Website: www.plowon.org
Office number: 361-588-7190

NOTES